THE UNIVERSE,
THE ELEVENTH DIMENSION,
AND EVERYTHING

THE UNIVERSE,
THE ELEVENTH DIMENSION,
AND EVERYTHING

WHAT WE KNOW AND HOW WE KNOW IT

RICHARD MORRIS

 FOUR WALLS EIGHT WINDOWS
New York · London

Published in the United States by
Four Walls Eight Windows
39 West 14th Street
New York, NY 10011
http://www.fourwallseightwindows.com

UK offices:
Four Walls Eight Windows/Turnaround
Unit 3 Olympia Trading Estate
Coburg Road, Wood Green
London N22 67Z

First printing October 1999.

LIBRARY OF CONGRESS CATALOGING-IN-PUBLICATION DATA:

Morris, Richard, 1939–
        The universe, the eleventh dimension, and everything : what we know and how we know it / Richard Morris.
            p.   cm..
        Includes index.
        ISBN 1-56858-140-8 (pbk.)
            1. Cosmology. 2. Unified field theories. 3. Life—Origin.
        I. Title.
        QB981.M8635   1999
        523.1—dc21   99-37643
                                                          CIP

Printed in Canada

10   9   8   7   6   5   4   3   2   1

CONTENTS

WHAT WE KNOW
AND HOW WE KNOW IT

During the last few years, there has been a series of exciting new discoveries in the fields of cosmology and particle physics, and scientists are at last beginning to understand the origin and evolution of the universe and the basic constituents of matter. These discoveries have been accompanied by a great deal of speculation. Scientists try not only to determine what is true, they also try to discover what might be true. Naturally there is nothing wrong with speculating in this manner. Before one can tell what the cosmos and the microworld are like, it is necessary to find out what the possibilities are.

Scientific knowledge has increased at such a rapid rate that some of this speculation has become quite astonishing. For example, scientists now have direct empirical evidence about the nature of the universe back to a time of about one second after the beginning of the big bang. This has led them to develop detailed theories about what might have been happening during that first second. Some have gone even further and have tried to invent plausible scenarios describing the creation of the universe. Others have wondered whether there might not be countless other universes besides our own.

Similarly, scientists have probed so deeply into the basic structure of matter that they are no longer content with discovering new subatomic particles and trying to understand their behavior. They are speculating about the nature of reality at an even more microscopic level, and attempting to probe into the very nature of space and time. They have begun to wonder if there might not be more dimensions of space than the three that we know, and have constructed theories about ten- and eleven-dimensional objects called superstrings and membranes.

One result of all this activity has been the publication of numerous books describing recent scientific speculation and discoveries. Ordinarily, great emphasis is given to the newest ideas. This is as it should be. Any book that failed to discuss them would quickly be out of date.

Many of the new ideas are quite appealing. If they are eventually confirmed, we will advance to new levels of scientific understanding, and our conceptions of both the universe and the microworld will be transformed. However, there are drawbacks associated with the emphasis on newly developed concepts that is characteristic of many books. The average, nonmathematically trained reader frequently finds it difficult to distinguish between scientific fact, partially confirmed hypotheses, and inspired guesses.

Thus I thought that it might not be a bad idea to write two little books (which appear as two sections of the book you are holding) outlining what we know about the universe and about the microworld with reasonable certainty. I decided, furthermore, that each of them should contain a brief, concluding outline of current speculation. If you understand precisely what is known, it is relatively easy to see why scientists should be trying to push the boundaries of knowledge outward in certain specific ways.

COSMIC EVOLUTION

When astronomers look 10 billion light years out into space, they are also looking 10 billion years back in time. As a result, they have been able to obtain a clear picture of the evolution of the universe from a time when it was very young. There are other kinds of observations that can be made that allow scientists to observe the universe when it was even younger. For example, the earth is bathed by radio waves coming from every direction of space. This *cosmic microwave background radiation* is made up of energy that was emitted in the form of bright light in the aftermath of the big bang, when the universe was about 300,000 years old. Over the course of billions of years, this light has been degraded into what are called microwaves (radio waves of short wavelength). Thus scientists can literally see the dying glow of the big bang.

I'll explain the nature and origin of this microwave background more fully in Part 1. For now, I only want to point out that it is possible to observe the universe as it was 12 billion years ago (12 billion years is a commonly used estimate of the universe's age). The scientists who study this radiation are literally looking back in time.

But 300,000 years does not represent a limit. Scientists have direct empirical evidence concerning the state of the universe down to a time of one second after its creation. Naturally, they cannot observe the early universe visually. Any light or other radiation that was emitted at a very early time would have been absorbed and re-emitted by the matter in the universe so many times that the chances of actually seeing what was going on are nil.

However, scientists can measure the quantities of certain chemical elements that could only have been created when the universe was very young. These elements cannot be created in stars; the high temperatures and energies in stellar interiors would have caused them to break apart as soon as they were made. Nuclei are broken up, as well as formed inside stars. Thus, by studying the abundances of these elements, astrophysicists are able to gain an understanding of the processes that were taking place when the universe was as young as one second old.

In Part 1, I will outline the evolution of the universe from a time of one second to the current era. Few scientists question the correctness of this picture. The story of cosmic evolution is not just theory. The underlying ideas have been checked against observations again and again.

Although the evolution of galaxies, stars, and planets is

a quite fascinating topic, I don't intend to stop there. One of the most obvious features of the universe is the fact that it contains life. The story of cosmic evolution does not end with the creation of life. The universe itself will eventually die, probably by becoming increasingly dark and cold. And it will almost certainly continue to change long after the last living organisms have died out. However, the existence of living beings is an important feature of the universe today. And it is a very surprising feature as well; in most of the possible universes that scientists are able to imagine, life could not exist.

UNDERSTANDING THE MICROWORLD

I will be taking a somewhat different approach when I outline what is known about the microworld. The reader will find little there about the properties of such fundamental objects as quarks (the constituents of protons, neutrons, and other heavy particles) and leptons (electrons and electronlike particles). The reason for this is a simple one: in order to understand current theoretical and experimental research about the microworld, it is necessary to know something about how current ideas originally developed.

For example, many physicists think that all fundamental particles may be made of superstrings, theoretical entities that are many orders of magnitude smaller then a proton, and which could not be seen even in particle accelerators that were millions or billions of times more powerful than the ones that now exist. Superstring theory depends upon the idea that there exist extra dimensions of space that are compacted or rolled up to such an extent that their existence probably could not be confirmed in any conceivable experiment.

But the possible existence of extra dimensions is not a new idea. It was first proposed during the 1930s. Shortly thereafter the concept drew the attention of Albert Einstein, and Einstein made use of it in his attempt to find a unified field theory, a theory that would explain both electromagnetism and gravity.

I imagine that many people wonder, when they first hear of superstrings, why scientists should devote so much time and effort to theorizing about entities that may forever remain undetectable, if indeed they do exist. The reason is that, if a successful superstring theory were found, then scientists would be able to include all four forces of nature—gravity, electromagnetism, and two distinct nuclear forces—within a single framework.

In order to understand why the goal of unification is so important, and why it has been sought by Einstein and by some of the most brilliant minds in physics today, it is necessary to know a little history. The quest for unification began during the nineteenth century when scientists began to try to understand the relationship between electricity and magnetism. The goal was reached when the Scottish physicist James Clerk Maxwell propounded a unified theory that explained both forces. But Maxwell's theory did much more than that; it also explained the nature of light and other kinds of radiation, and led to the discovery of radio waves.

When two or more theories are melded into one, the combined theory often turns out to be much more than the proverbial sum of its parts. New kinds of phenomena are frequently predicted. Maxwell's electromagnetic theory is an especially dramatic example. Its discovery led, not only to a deeper understanding of the nature of physical reality, but also to many of the technological innovations upon which modern life depends.

The quest for unification has not always been a major preoccupation of physicists. In fact, by the middle of the twentieth century, it was forgotten by every prominent physicist but Einstein. To many of them, Einstein's quest for a unified theory was a quixotic endeavor, and it caused him to become isolated from his colleagues.

[5]

There were reasons for this neglect. Many physicists believed, with good justification, that it was necessary first to discover what subatomic particles existed, and to understand the forces that influenced their behavior. The nature of the *strong* nuclear force, the one that held protons and neutrons together in atomic nuclei, proved to be especially baffling. Although the atomic nucleus was discovered in 1911 and although it was known to consist of protons and neutrons by 1932, it wasn't until the 1970s that scientists were able to develop a workable theory of the forces that held nuclei together. Before then, they were forced to work with various different approximations. It was often necessary to use one approximation in some cases and a second approximation in others.

It was only after scientists understood the nature of each of the four forces that a quest for unification began anew. However problems appeared immediately. Gravity was explained by Einstein's general theory of relativity and the other three forces by quantum mechanics. Both theories seemed to be well confirmed. However, they were also mutually contradictory. There seemed to be no way that they could be combined into a single theory of all four forces.

And then superstring theory was discovered. Although there was no empirical evidence to support its basic ideas, it was a theory that seemed to be capable of explaining all four forces within a single framework. Some physicists were extremely skeptical about it. But others felt that it was too logical not to be true. Recently, scientists have been exploring something called membrane or *brane* theory, which incorporates ideas about superstrings within a larger framework. As I write this, neither superstring nor brane theory has been experimentally confirmed, and no one knows when or how it might be. Physics has caught sight of what has been described as a "holy grail." But the grail has remained tantalizingly out of reach.

[6]

In this chapter, too, I will be outlining what is known with near certainty before I embark on a brief discussion of current speculation. But the exposition will be a little different. Ideas about the nature of the microworld have been evolving for about a century. During that time, certain scientific approaches (such as the idea of extra dimensions of space) have been investigated, discarded, and then reinvented. I believe that the best way to comprehend what is happening at the frontiers of physics is to learn how currently fashionable ideas came about. It is often necessary to know the past in order to understand the present, even in the physical sciences.

THE SCIENTIFIC IMAGINATION

There exists no experimental or observational data to support some of the currently popular ideas about the evolution of the universe during the first second, or about the fundamental nature of matter. How, then, can one call such speculation *scientific?* It would seem that there is more empirical support for such things as astrology and parapsychology, which scientists generally consider to be pseudosciences.

This is not an easy question to answer. Consequently I will devote the entire last section of the book to exploring the nature of the scientific imagination, and of scientific discovery. My approach will not be a philosophical one. Like many physicists, I don't find philosophical discussions of the nature of scientific knowledge, or of scientific methods, to be very relevant. There is no scientific method. Scientists, and especially physicists, make use of any method that will work.

What I propose to do instead is to look at the working of scientific minds in detail. Along the way, I will explain why such endeavors as theoretical research in superstring theory are scientific while the disciplines commonly regarded as pseudosciences are not. I will discuss certain important scientific discoveries, and examine the methods used by the scientists who made those discoveries. You may find some of my conclusions to be a bit surprising. For example, I think that it can be shown that style and personality can play as important a role in science as in art.

Since I want to emphasize this again—my approach will not be a philosophical one, I may not always reach firm conclusions. The scientific imagination is a topic that I want to explore, not systemize. For me, this exploration will be the most interesting part of this book. I hope that the reader will agree.

COSMIC EVOLUTION

PREFACE

Anyone who reads a book on cosmology these days is likely to encounter a great deal of talk about speculative theories. The authors who write on the subject generally devote a lot of space to such matters as alternate universes, cosmic wormholes, the origin of the universe as a quantum fluctuation, and the physical processes that were taking place when the universe was 10^{-35} (a hundred-millionth of a billionth of a billionth of a billionth) seconds old.

Much of this speculation is extremely interesting. Indeed, I have written about it at length myself. However, it has occurred to me that there might be a place for a description of what we know about the universe with something like 99 percent confidence or better. Scientific knowledge advances rapidly these days, and most books that deal with research at the frontiers of physics and cosmology become out of date in less than five years. Thus it might be interesting to describe the scientific knowledge that is not likely to be overthrown in the immediate or intermediate future.

The matters that I will discuss are not speculation; they are based on solid observational evidence. We know, for example, that there was a big bang. There are a number of different kinds of evidence that support this theory of the origin of the universe, and it is not likely that they could be explained away. Furthermore, scientists know what the universe was like back to a time of about one second after it was created. Certain kinds of atomic nuclei exist today that could only have been created in the early universe. It is possible to measure the quantities of these nuclei that are present, not only in our solar system, but also in distant galaxies. This gives us information about what conditions must have been like when those galaxies were formed. We know that the universe is filled with a substance that scientists call *dark matter*. Though dark matter cannot be seen in any telescope, its gravitational effects can be observed and measured. Finally, scientists have a pretty good idea as to how the universe will evolve in the future. There is every reason to believe that Einstein's theory of gravitation, his general theory of relativity, is correct; and it can be used to calculate the state of the universe as it was billions of years ago, and to determine what the universe will be like long after intelligent life ceases to exist.

Many accounts of the evolution of the universe go back to a much earlier time than one second. But they all depend upon an assumption that has never been proven, that Einstein's theory remains valid when gravitational fields become very intense. There is every reason to think that it does. However, general relativity has only been tested in relatively weak gravitational fields, such as those that are found near the surface of the earth or of the sun. Thus, though the extrapolation to times earlier than one second probably yields valid results, there is no empirical evidence to confirm that this is in fact the case. Authors who write about the very early universe, therefore, are dealing with matters that cannot be described with anything approaching certainty.

The evolution of the universe since a time of one second is well understood. For example, physicists have been studying nuclear physics since the 1930s, and there is every reason to believe that their ideas about the reactions that go on inside our sun and other stars are perfectly accurate. Scientists also know how stars evolve. Astronomers can observe stars in all stages of evolution. They see very young stars, middle-aged stars (of which our sun is an example), stars that are undergoing their death throes, and stars that ceased to produce any energy long ago, and which are now only dim remnants that glow only because they have a certain amount of residual heat.

Astrophysicists understand the details of how the chemical elements were created and spread throughout space. It has been established that only very light elements, such as helium and traces of lithium, were created in the big bang fireball. All of the others are the end products of nuclear reactions that take place within stars. These elements were spread through space in supernova explosions. It is possible to say that we, and our planet, are composed primarily of cosmic debris.

Some details of galaxy formation are, as yet, only imperfectly understood. However, it is possible to describe the creation of galaxies in a general way, and to explain why some galaxies look very much different from others. Explaining the formation of stars and planets presents no problems. We can even say how it happened that the earth is so hospitable to life. The precise nature of the first living organisms is something that is still argued about. But then that topic is part of biology, not of cosmology or physics.

There are not very many unanswered questions remaining about the evolution of the universe from a time of one second to the present day. Ideas about where the universe came from may be speculative in nature, but the story of cosmic evolution is not. The telling of this story will constitute the greater part of this section.

I don't plan to ignore less well-established ideas entirely. After I summarize what we know about the evolution of the universe, I will comment on some recent ideas that are very probably—although not certainly—true. I think it is important to explain why contemporary scientists believe it should be possible to theorize about matters that cannot be supported by direct empirical evidence. They believe—with a great deal of justification—that if theory proves to be correct up to a certain point, then it ought to be possible to go a little further. It is only when theory leaves observation far behind that we enter the realm of pure speculation.

CHAPTER 1
THE BEGINNING

Like the impressionist movement in painting, the big bang theory of the origin of the universe was given its name by a hostile critic. On a radio broadcast in 1950, the English astronomer Fred Hoyle derisively referred to the *big bang* theory. According to the rival steady state theory of the universe, which had been proposed by Hoyle and physicists Thomas Gold and Hermann Bondi, the universe had no beginning in time; it had always existed.

Today, of course, we know that there was a beginning. The universe came into existence some 10 to 15 billion years ago. It was initially in a very hot, highly compressed state, and it has been expanding ever since. Although it is impossible to say what was happening at time zero, we know that when the universe was one second old many of the atomic nuclei that exist today were already being formed. At the time, the universe was a hot, glowing fireball, and was rapidly cooling as it expanded.

FIG. 1: *The expansion of the universe. The concept of an expanding universe can be understood by making an analogy with a rising loaf of raisin bread. Here, the loaf represents the universe, and the raisins are galaxies or clusters of galaxies. As the raisin bread rises, the distance between the raisins becomes greater, and each one seems to move away from all the others. The difference, of course, is that a loaf of bread increases in volume only very slightly, while the expansion of the universe has been enormous.*

There are three kinds of evidence that enable scientists to reach this conclusion. The first of the three is probably the weakest: the fact that the universe is expanding today. Observations of distant galaxies show that galaxies and clusters of galaxies are moving apart. It seems only reasonable to suppose that there must have been a time when all of the matter in the universe was compressed in a small space. But this piece of evidence is not conclusive. It is possible to devise theories in which the universe did not originate with a big bang, but is expanding nevertheless. In fact, this is precisely what Hoyle, Gold, and Bondi proposed. They knew very well that the universe was expanding, but they assumed that, as it did, new matter was created in intergalactic space. In time, this matter would accumulate, and new galaxies would be formed. They were thus able to avoid the problem of a beginning. To be sure, no one had ever seen matter pop into existence. However, the steady state theory required only that one new hydrogen atom be created in each cubic meter of space once every 10 billion years. The proposed rate of creation was much too small to be observable.

THE COSMIC MICROWAVE BACKGROUND

A lot of scientists found the idea of a steady state universe to be appealing. The theory avoided the problem of having to explain how the universe began. According to Hoyle, Gold, and Bondi, it had always existed. However, the theory was discredited in 1964 when two Bell Laboratories radio astronomers, Arno Penzias and Robert Wilson, discovered that microwaves—short radio waves—were falling on the earth from every direction. The intensity of the microwave radiation was the same in every section of the sky Penzias and Wilson examined, and it did not vary according to the hour of the day or night.

Many years previously, the Russian-American physicist

George Gamow had predicted that, if the big bang theory were correct, then the earth should be bathed with microwave radiation like that which was discovered by Penzias and Wilson. In 1949, together with his students Ralph Alpher and Robert Herman, he had published a paper in which he predicted that it should be possible to observe a relic of the big bang in the form of blackbody radiation with a temperature of about 5 degrees Kelvin (degrees Celsius above absolute zero). By the time that Penzias and Wilson made their discovery, the work of Gamow and his students had been forgotten. However, a group of cosmologists working at Princeton University consisting of physicist Robert Dicke and his colleagues had rediscovered Gamow's result.

I think a few words of explanation are in order. For example, it may not be obvious to the lay reader why the radiation should have been coming from everywhere, not from some specific direction in space. The reason is that the big bang was not an explosion that expanded outward into some pre-existing space. On the contrary, it filled the entire universe. When scientists speak of the universe as something that is expanding, they mean that space itself expands, carrying galaxies along with it. Nothing exists outside the universe; according to the general theory of relativity, there is no such thing as *outside* (a point that I will discuss in more detail somewhat later). Radiation from the big bang comes from everywhere because the big bang happened everywhere.

Blackbody radiation is radiation that is emitted by a perfectly black object, one that absorbs all the light or other radiation that falls upon it. True blackbodies do not exist in nature; every known material reflects some light. However, it is possible to produce a simulation of a blackbody in the laboratory, and to study the radiation that it emits when it is heated. The characteristics of blackbody radiation are thus well understood.

[16]

The big bang fireball was extraordinarily bright and hot. So why should we see radio waves today? There are several ways of approaching this question. Perhaps the simplest is to make an analogy with the behavior of a hot object as it cools. If a white hot piece of iron is allowed to cool, its color will turn from white to red. As it cools further, it will cease to emit visible light, but will emit invisible infrared radiation. No matter how much it cools, it will emit radiation of some kind. If it is cooled to a temperature of a few degrees above absolute zero, it emits microwaves. This is directly correlated with temperature. Microwaves are less energetic than infrared radiation, which is less energetic than visible light. Since less energy is released at a lower temperature, it stands to reason that it should be given off a different form.

The universe was created 10 to 15 billion years ago, and it has been cooling ever since. When the light from the big bang fireball was emitted, the universe had a radiation temperature of about 3000 degrees Kelvin. It has a temperature of about -270 degrees Celsius today. Scientists generally express this as 3 degrees Kelvin, since absolute zero, the temperature at which all molecular motion ceases, is -273 degrees C (the radiation temperature is actually known quite precisely; the exact figure is 2.726 degrees). This doesn't quite agree with Gamow's prediction of a 5 degree temperature, but his estimate was remarkably close for 1949.

Observing the microwave background radiation allows scientists to see the universe as it was when it was only 300,000 years old. We know that the radiation was emitted at that time because the temperature of the universe was previously too high for electrons to form atoms by attaching themselves to hydrogen and helium nuclei. There was so much radiation energy in the universe that atoms would have been broken apart as soon as they formed. This prevented light from traveling any great distances. Light rays interacted with free electrons before they were able to travel very far. If there had been any sentient beings in those days, they would have perceived the universe as something that was shrouded in a dense fog. But when the temperature fell to about 3000 degrees, these electrons became parts of atoms, and light was able to travel about unimpeded. The fog suddenly disipated.

When I say that observations of the microwave background radiation allow us to see the universe as it was when it was 300,000 years old, I am not speaking metaphorically. In 1992, apparatus that had been placed on the Cosmic Background Explorer (COBE) satellite was able to take a picture of the universe as it appeared at that time. Furthermore, the satellite experiment detected temperature fluctuations in the microwave radiation. This was precisely what cosmologists had expected. If certain regions of the universe had not contained a little more matter than others, the universe would not have the character that it possesses today. As we shall see, the creation of galaxies depended upon the existence of regions that were slightly denser than average. Scientists realized that, if such regions existed, they would emit more radiation than others. Failure to detect such fluctuations would have indicated that there was something seriously wrong with the big bang theory.

PRIMORDIAL HELIUM AND DEUTERIUM

If the best that we could do was to determine what the universe was like at an age of about 300,000 years, trying to understand what was going on before that time would involve a lot of guesswork. However, it is not necessary to make guesses. Scientists can, in fact, *see* the universe at an age of one second. It was at this time that certain light atomic nuclei began to be created. Measurements of the quantities of these nuclei that exist today provide direct observational evidence about the early universe.

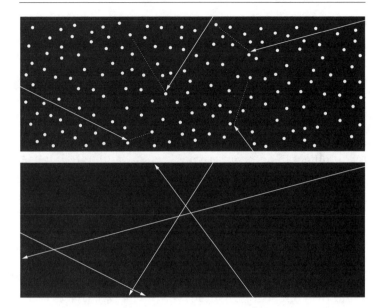

FIG. 2: *The primeval fog. Before the universe was about 300,000 years old, rays of light could not travel very far before they were scattered, or absorbed, by electrons. If any observers had been present to see it, space would have had the appearance of being filled with a dense fog. But then the universe cooled sufficiently to allow the electrons to combine with hydrogen and helium nuclei to form atoms, and light could pass through space quite freely. The radiation from the big bang fireball that we see today originated when the universe suddenly became transparent.*

Originally, the universe contained only basic particles of matter such as protons, neutrons, and electrons. Then, when it had reached an age of about one second, helium nuclei began to be created in large quantities. A helium nucleus consists of two protons and two neutrons. It was formed from the protons and neutrons that existed in the early universe. The helium that scientists observe today could not have been created in stars. Although 10 to 15 billion years have passed since the universe began, there has not been enough time for stars to create the quantities of helium that are seen. At best, the nuclear reactions that take place within stars could have created only about 10 or 15 percent of the helium that is known to exist.

Measuring the chemical composition of stars, galaxies, and of interstellar or intergalactic gas is not very difficult. Each chemical element emits light at certain characteristic wavelengths when it is heated, and it is only necessary to study the light (or radio waves in the case of gas) emitted by an object to determine what it is made of. When these measurements are performed, it is found that the universe is about 25 percent helium and about 75 percent hydrogen by weight. All of the other elements exist only in relatively small quantities.

The nuclear reactions that take place within stars are well understood, and it is possible to calculate the quantities of helium that they have produced. It is impossible to avoid the conclusion that most of the helium that is seen must have come from somewhere else. That *somewhere else* could only have been the big bang fireball. This line of reasoning is confirmed by the fact that smaller quantities of helium are found in older stars. Old stars generally contain 2 to 3 percent less helium than our sun, which was formed only 5 billion years ago.

DEUTERON HELIUM

FIG. 3: *The deuteron and the helium nucleus. Deuterium has a nucleus that is made up of one proton and one neutron. The two particles can be separated from one another relatively easily. The helium nucleus, which is made up of two protons and two neutrons, is much more stable. A great deal of energy is required to break it apart into its component particles.*

Conditions in the early universe can be determined in several different ways. For example, trace amounts of deuterium exist in the universe. Deuterium is an isotope of hydrogen; it has the same chemical behavior that hydrogen has, but a different number of particles in its nucleus. A hydrogen atom consists of a single proton that is orbited by a single electron. A deuterium nucleus consists of a proton and a neutron. Since the electrical charge is the same in either case only a single negatively charged electron will attach itself to the nucleus.

Deuterium cannot be made in stars. The proton and neutron are too weakly bound to one another. If any deuterium is formed in a star, the high temperatures will cause it to quickly break apart. Since deuterium cannot come from stars, it must have been created in the big bang fireball, where conditions were somewhat different. To be sure, some deuterium nuclei were broken up at that time. However, the universe cooled rapidly during the early stages of its expansion and many deuterium nuclei survived.

Finally, a few other light nuclei were created in the big bang in trace amounts. These include helium-3 (two neutrons and a proton), lithium-6 (three neutrons and three protons), and lithium-7 (four neutrons and three protons). None of the heavier elements were created at this time. The necessary conditions for their formation did not exist.

Nucleosynthesis—the creation of light atomic nuclei—took place when the universe was about one second to three minutes old. After that these processes stopped. The temperature of the universe had fallen to the point that the energy required to stick subnuclear particles together was no longer available. And of course the energy required to break nuclei like deuterium apart just wasn't there either. A deuterium nucleus can be split if it undergoes a collision with another particle. But if the other particles, or the radiation that is present, do not possess enough energy to make this happen, it survives. There is, of course, a relation between temperature and the energy of individual particles. For example, the temperature of an object encountered in everyday life is a consequence of the motion of its constituent molecules. In the early universe, temperature is measured by the motion of energetic particles (e.g., protons and neutrons) instead.

We thus possess two "snapshots" of the early universe, a time exposure taken when it was one second to three minutes old, and another at an age of 300,000 years. It is not very difficult to imagine what was happening in between. No complicated processes took place. The universe simply cooled and expanded.

Scientists also possess pictures of the universe at various times since the cosmic background radiation was emitted. When astronomers study distant objects, they are looking back in time. When they observe a galaxy 10 billion light years away, they see 10 billion years into the past. This follows from the definition of the term *light year*, the distance that a ray of light travels in one year (a light year is about 6 trillion miles). Thus scientists are able to observe the galaxies that formed a billion or two years after the big bang, and they can study galaxies as they appeared in more recent times. They have seen old stars that are almost as old as the universe, young stars that are only a few hundred thousand years old. They have looked at regions where star formation is taking place right now, and at others where star formation occurred long ago. By looking back in time, they can see the universe in various stages of its evolution.

THE VERY EARLY UNIVERSE

One thing that scientists cannot do is observe the evolution of the universe before a time of one second. They must depend upon theory instead. However, there is a point at which all theories break down. Newton's law of gravitation cannot accurately describe the things that happen when gravity is very intense. Scientists must use the general theory of relativity instead. However, general relativity breaks down too when quantum effects become important. It is incompatible with quantum mechanics, the theory which is used to describe the behavior of subatomic particles.

In fact, if one attempts to use general relativity to extrapolate all the way back to the beginning of the universe, one obtains a result that is nonsense. It is possible to prove mathematically that if general relativity is a correct theory, then the universe must have begun in a state of infinite matter density. Now, whenever an infinity appears in a theory, this is generally a sign that something has gone terribly wrong. In fact, the impossibility of infinite quantities is sometimes used to prove certain results. According to Einstein's special theory of relativity, the theory that describes the behavior of objects that are traveling at high velocities, an infinite quantity of energy would be required to accelerate an object to the speed of light. This is generally taken to be a proof that no material object can ever travel at light velocity.

If we wanted to know what was happening at the moment of the creation of the universe, a theory of quantum gravity, one which combined quantum mechanics and relativity would be required. But no such theory has ever been found. Theories about the origin of the universe must therefore be of a speculative nature.

Many physicists believe that general relativity accurately describes the evolution of the universe back to a time of 10^{-43} seconds after the beginning.[1] This is the time when quantum effects would have ceased to be important. When I speak of *quantum effects* I am not referring to the gravitational effects of whatever high-energy particles were present, but of alterations in the very nature of space and time. If quantum mechanics is a correct theory—and there is no reason to think that it is not—then space and time must originally have had a character somewhat different than that which is observed today. Unfortunately, no one knows what these alterations of space and time were like, only that they should have existed for a short moment after the universe was born.

There is also another note of uncertainty. As I noted previously, general relativity has never been tested in gravitational fields like those that presumably existed at early times. Gravity of that strength simply does not exist in the present day universe. Thus any theory that attempts to describe the universe at very early times must make use of an unproven idea, that general relativity will continue to be valid whenever quantum effects are unimportant. Scientists know of no reason why general relativity should break down before that point is reached. However, using it under such circumstances requires an act of faith.

The best-known theory of the early universe is the inflationary universe theory, which was discovered by the Massachusetts Institute of Technology physicist Alan Guth in 1979. According to Guth, the universe underwent a period of extraordinarily rapid expansion when it was 10^{-35} to 10^{-33} seconds old.[2] During that time, an enormous repulsive force existed in the universe, causing it to *inflate* to a much larger size. During this period, the volume of the universe doubled once every 10^{-35} seconds. Today the universe doubles in size about once every 10 billion years.

Since the inflationary expansion presumably took place long before a time of one second, it is impossible to perform observations that might confirm or falsify it. Nevertheless the inflationary theory is widely accepted by scientists. They know of no other theory that can explain why the universe possesses the characteristics that it has today. For example, when the universe was one second old, it had to have a matter density that was equal to a certain figure to an accuracy of fifteen decimal places. If the density had been greater than this by even a tiny amount, then gravity would have caused the expansion of the universe to cease relatively quickly. A state of contraction would have ensued, and the universe would have collapsed in a *big crunch* long before life had a chance to evolve. If the density had been less than the critical figure by a tiny amount, then the expansion would have proceeded so rapidly that stars and galaxies could never have formed. Matter would have been flying apart at too great a velocity.

Now it turns out that, if the inflationary universe theory is correct, the universe would have had exactly the right density. The rapid expansion that began at a time of 10^{-35} seconds would have fine-tuned the density of the universe in just the right way. The rapid expansion would have brought about exactly the matter density that was needed. This may sound like some kind of mathematical sleight of hand. But it really isn't. When the equations associated with the inflationary theory are worked out in detail, it turns out that it doesn't matter very much what the density originally was.

I don't propose to discuss the inflationary universe theory in any great detail. Fuller descriptions of the theory can be found in many books, including Alan Guth's excellent *The Inflationary Universe* (Addison Wesley, 1997), and some of my own books as well. My only purpose in discussing Guth's theory is to make a comparison between the universe that we can observe and the universe we can only theorize about. We know what has been happening since a time of one second because our knowledge is based on things that can be seen and measured. Descriptions of the universe before a time of one second, on the other hand, are purely theoretical.

THE ROAD AHEAD

In the remainder of this part, I will discuss the evolution of the universe from a time of one second to the present day. Most of the topics covered will lie in the fields of astronomy, cosmology, and astrophysics. But not all of them will be. I believe that the story of cosmic evolution would be incomplete without any mention of the evolution of life. Life, after all, is the greatest mystery of all. Scientists are able to visualize many different kinds of possible universes. In most of them, life would never have the chance to evolve. So why is it that our universe is so hospitable to living beings? As we shall see, the creation of life is part of the story of cosmic evolution.

NOTES

[1] Scientists generally use what is called exponential notation to write large numbers. For example 1 million can be written as 10^6 which is the numeral 1 followed by six zeros. 10^{43} is 1 followed by forty-three zeros; it is equal to 10 million trillion trillion trillion. 10^{-43} is 1 divided by 10^{43}. To call it microscopically small would be a gross understatement.

[2] Recall that 10^{-33} is a larger number than 10^{-35}.

CHAPTER 2

WHEN THE UNIVERSE WAS
ONE SECOND OLD

When the universe was one second old, it contained protons, neutrons, electrons, and light particles called neutrinos. There was about one neutron for every ten protons. No atoms existed at this time. The temperature—nearly 10 billion degrees Kelvin—was so high that any electron that attached itself to a proton to form a hydrogen atom would have immediately been kicked away by the radiation that permeated the universe.

If left to itself, a neutron will decay in about ten minutes, producing a proton, an electron, and a neutrino.[1] However, the density of matter in the early universe was so great that most of the neutrons did not have time to decay; they collided with protons before this happened. When these collisions took place, deuterium nuclei were frequently created. A deuterium nucleus, which, as you will recall, consists of a proton and a neutron, is also called *heavy hydrogen*.

Many of the deuterium nuclei then collided with neutrons to form tritium, a nucleus that consists of two neutrons and a proton. Finally, the addition of another proton to these nuclei created helium. A helium nucleus consists of two protons and two neutrons, and is said to have a mass of four. Since the neutron and the proton are nearly equal in weight, it is possible to assign a mass number of 1 to each. In this scheme, neutrons and protons each have mass 1, deuterium has mass 2, and tritium mass 3. The helium nucleus, which has mass 4, is the most stable of the compound nuclei.

These nuclear reactions continued until the universe was about three minutes old. After that time, the energy required to create new kinds of nuclei was no longer present. Gasses cool when they expand, as anyone who has ever used an aerosol can knows. When expanding gas is released, the can begins to feel cool to the hand. Lower temperatures meant that the subatomic particles that filled the universe had less energy. As a result, nuclear reactions could no longer take place.

When the universe was three minutes old, it was made up of a little less then 75 percent hydrogen. Here, when I say *hydrogen* I mean hydrogen nuclei, or protons. Atoms did not yet exist, but astrophysicists habitually say *hydrogen* to mean hydrogen nuclei. Most of the remaining matter consisted of helium. Although the creation of deuterium is one of the steps in the formation of helium, very little of the former remained. The reason for this is that deuterium is not very stable; the proton and the neutron that are its components are weakly bound. But, where deuterium can easily be broken apart, helium is very stable. It takes a lot of energy to pry it apart. Tritium is also less stable than helium, which tended to be the end product of the reactions that took place in the early universe.

A little tritium and lithium (mass 7) also existed then, and are still observed today. But the heavier elements did not. There was no carbon, no nitrogen, no oxygen, and no iron or other metals. There was no way that these could have been created in the big bang fireball. The reason is that there is no stable element of mass 5, or of mass 8. When a proton or a neutron encountered a helium nucleus, nothing very significant happened. Similarly, if two helium nuclei encountered one another, they simply wouldn't have stuck together. And if this didn't happen, the heavier elements could not be created.

During the early days of the big bang theory, it had been believed that all of the elements could have been synthesized in the big bang. In 1946, George Gamow had published a paper suggesting that this might be possible. At the time, the idea seemed reasonable enough. However, as knowledge of nuclear physics increased, it became apparent that Gamow's scheme was impossible. The heavier elements had to have been created in some other manner. Today we know how this happened. But perhaps it would be best if I didn't digress too much here. The synthesis of the heavy elements is a topic that I will be discussing later.

THE FORMATION OF GALAXIES AND STARS

When the universe was 300,000 years old, it contained little but hydrogen and helium gas. But the gas was not of uniform density. There were some regions in which the concentrations were slightly higher and others in which it was lower. These variations in density were not large. Variations of the order of one part in 100,000 would have been sufficient to produce the galaxies and clusters of galaxies that we see today.

Everything in the universe feels the effect of gravity. Now, gravity is a very weak force compared to the others that we know of. If you doubt this, consider the fact that a small magnet can be used to pick up an iron or steel object. In this case the magnetic forces are greater than the gravitational force exerted by the entire earth. However gravity is a long-range force, and it never ceases to act. Consequently, it was much more important than another forces that existed at the time. Gravity caused the denser-than-average regions to expand a little more slowly than the rest of the universe. Gravitational attraction drew more matter into these regions, and they became denser yet. This process went on for countless millions of years until the gas clouds became dense and concentrated enough that they began to contract.

As the contraction continued, according to the most popular scenario for galaxy formation, the clouds began to fragment into smaller clouds that were to eventually become galaxies. Finally, the density of matter in certain regions of the daughter clouds became great enough that stars began to form within them. By a time of about 1 billion years after the big bang, stars were beginning to light up the sky.

This picture of galaxy formation is called the *top-down* scenario. It is meant to explain the fact that galaxies are typically found in clusters. Our own Milky Way galaxy, for example, is a member of a cluster of some twenty-odd galaxies, called the local group, that also includes the great galaxy in Andromeda. The galaxies in the group are held together by gravity, and individual members orbit around one another in complicated ways. The local group is quite a small cluster compared to some that astronomers have observed. Some of these superclusters contain about a thousand galaxies each.

There is also a *bottom-up* scenario in which the galaxies formed first and clusters of galaxies were created later when gravity brought the individual members together. The top-down theory seems to work a little better than its competitor. Hence it is favored by most cosmologists. However, the difference between these two scenarios is not as great as one might think. In both of them galaxies are formed in the same manner. The only thing that is different is the manner of cluster formation.

The first stars were formed by a very similar mechanism. As the protogalaxies contracted, they too began to break into fragments. Gravity caused the fragments to contract still further and to become very hot; just as expanding gasses cool, compressed gasses increase in temperature. Eventually the fragments became so hot that nuclear fusion began within their cores. Hydrogen was converted into helium in a manner similar to the way that hydrogen converts to helium in an H bomb. The nuclear reactions responsible for the fusion can take place only at high temperatures. This is why hydrogen bombs have atomic bomb triggers. Of course there are significant differences between the fusion that takes place within a star and that in a bomb. A star burns its nuclear fuel steadily rather than igniting at once.

The steps involved in the creation of a new star are somewhat complicated, and I won't go into all the details. It should be sufficient to describe the broad outlines of the process. At first, a protostar is able to radiate away most of the heat created by contraction. But in the later stages of star formation, this heat is confined within the star's core. The star has become too dense for heat to escape easily. If a protostar is large enough, nuclear reactions will eventually begin. If it is not large enough, it will become what is known as a brown dwarf. The planet Jupiter is one such "failed star." Though it was formed billions of years ago, it is still contracting at a slow rate and radiating away more energy than it receives from the sun. If Jupiter had been a bit larger, and if the pressure and temperature in its core had been greater, it would have ignited, and ours would be a binary star system.

THE FIRST STARS

It is thought that the first stars were large and massive, perhaps 10 times heavier and 10,000 times as bright as our sun. Nuclear reactions take place rapidly in stars of this size, and they have short lifetimes, of perhaps 10 million years. By comparison, our sun, which is an average-size star, has been shining for approximately 5 billion years. Another 5 billion will pass before it exhausts its nuclear fuel.

The oldest stars that astronomers see, which have an age of about 12 billion years, have a heavy element abundance that is about 1 percent of that found in our sun. One percent doesn't sound like very much, but it is an indication that these could not have been among the first stars to be formed. As we have seen, heavy elements could not have been created in the big bang; they had to come from somewhere else. And, as we shall see, these elements are formed in the cores of massive, short-lived stars, which eject these elements into space when they reach the end of their lives.

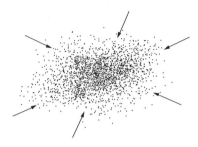

FIG. 4: *The creation of stars and galaxies. The two processes are similar. If a cloud of gas has higher-than-average density, gravitational forces (here represented by the arrows) will cause it to contract and to become denser yet. This will cause the gravitational force to become even greater. However, there is a limit to how far the contraction will continue. If a galaxy is rotating, there will be a point where the force of gravity is balanced by centrifugal forces. Then contraction can continue no further. But denser-than-average gas clouds within the galaxy can contract to form stars.*

An earlier generation of stars must have preceded the oldest ones that we see today. Since these stars must have been born, and have burned out and died before the later stars were formed, they must have had short lives. Twelve billion years, after all, is close to the age of the universe, and there exist second-generation stars of that age. If the first stars burned out quickly, they must have been very large. No one knows exactly how big they were, but the figure of ten times the mass of the sun that I cited previously seems like a very good guess. The reason that our sun contains quantities of heavy elements that are a hundred times as great can be attributed to the fact that it is only 5 billion years old. By the time it was formed, more than one generation of stars had burned out and died, and heavy elements were present in the universe in greater abundance.

WHITE DWARFS, RED GIANTS, AND SUPERNOVAS

To understand what happens when a massive star dies, it is best to begin by considering the fate of a star the size of our sun. Like most stars, the sun obtains its energy from reactions that convert hydrogen to helium within its core. Helium nuclei have masses that are about seven-tenths of a percent less than that of four protons. There is only one thing that can happen to the mass that disappears during this reaction; it is converted into energy. According to Einstein's famous equation $E = mc^2$, mass and energy are equivalent. Here, c is the speed of light, which is 10 billion centimeters per second in the metric units that scientists use; c^2, the speed of light multiplied by itself, is thus a huge number, which indicates that a small quantity of mass is equivalent to a large amount of energy. You shouldn't be puzzled by the fact that the speed of light comes into the equation. The quantity c^2 is only a conversion factor.

Nothing lasts forever, and the sun's supply of nuclear fuel will eventually run out. At first, less energy and heat will be produced, and the sun will begin to contract under the influence of gravity as the pressure produced by the nuclear reactions in its core begins to drop. Even though the nuclear reaction's core will be producing less heat than previously, the temperature of the core will begin to rise. This is analogous to the process that causes a star to become hot in its early stages of formation. In both cases, compression produces heat.

When the temperature becomes high enough, the helium in the sun will begin to burn. Two helium nuclei can fuse to become one of the metal beryllium, which has a mass of 8. Now it so happens that beryllium 8 is unstable.[2] If left to itself, it will quickly split apart into two helium nuclei again. However, if it collides with a third helium nucleus before this happens, carbon (mass number 12) will be formed.

[33]

In very massive stars, similar processes will take place and oxygen and other elements heavier than carbon will be created. The core of our sun, however, will never become hot enough for this to happen. Carbon will be the end product of its reactions.

Helium burning produces a lot of energy. As strange as it sounds, this will cause the sun to heat up and cool at the same time. As the core becomes hotter, the outer layers of the sun will expand, and cool as they do. The sun will grow to a size of about 100 times its present radius. As it does, it will become red; an object that glows red hot is cooler than one that glows white.

Eventually the helium fuel will be exhausted too. In fact, the sun will use up its helium at a much more rapid rate than it exhausted its hydrogen. This is a consequence of the fact that the energy production during the red giant stage is higher. The helium burning will continue for only about 100 million years, or about 1 percent of the time required for the sun to use up its hydrogen. When this happens, the sun will begin to cool, and to shrink into an object called a white dwarf. The core will no longer be generating enough heat to provide the pressure needed to hold up the sun's outer layers. The sun will continue to glow, but this will be a consequence of its residual heat, not of any nuclear reactions that are taking place.

White dwarfs can continue to glow for 10 billion years before they fade away completely and become black dwarfs. Since 10 billion years is a span of time nearly as great as the age of the universe, white dwarfs should be quite common. And indeed they are. Astronomers have discovered countless numbers of them.

When a star like the sun shrinks into a white dwarf, there is a lower limit to its size. Eventually the electrons within the star will be squeezed together so tightly that further contraction will be impossible. The dying star will be held up by what is called *electron degeneracy pressure* in the language of quantum mechanics. Quantum mechanics makes it possible for scientists to compute the densities of white dwarfs quite accurately. When the sun becomes a white dwarf, it will have a diameter that is about 1 percent of the present value, and it will be so compressed that it will have a density about a million times as great as that of terrestrial rock.

Quantum mechanics also tells us that there is a limit to how large a white dwarf can be. If it has a mass more than 1.4 times that of the sun, gravitational forces will be so great that the electron degeneracy pressure will no longer be able to hold the star up. Again, there is a visual way of thinking about a process that physicists describe with abstruse mathematical equations. We can picture the star's electrons as being "squeezed" into the protons, creating neutrons. The star will then shrink until the neutrons are packed together as tightly as they will go. A neutron star is the result. Neutrons stars do not glow the way that white dwarfs do. But they have been detected. They emit radio waves, for example, and these can be observed. When the first neutron star was discovered in 1967, scientists thought at first that they might be receiving signals from an extraterrestrial civilization. The radio signals soon proved to be too regular to permit this interpretation, however. They were pulses 0.016 seconds in length that arrived once every 1.337 seconds. This regularity indicated that they were coming from a natural object, which proved to be a neutron star that was spinning rapidly while giving off radio waves in a specific direction. Every 1.337 second, its radio signal would flash by us like a lighthouse beacon.

If a white dwarf can have a weight of no more than 1.4 solar masses, it does not follow that it evolved from a star of that size. All stars throw off considerable quantities of matter when they reach the ends of their lives. A star may have a mass as much as eight times that of the sun, and still evolve into a white dwarf. Stars that are more massive than this evolve into neutron stars or black holes. A black hole is created when the remnants of a dead star are so massive that not even the neutron degeneracy pressure can hold it up. All of the matter in the star then collapses into a volume approaching that of a mathematical point. Scientists do not really know what happens in the final stages of collapse because when the matter in the star becomes too dense, Einstein's general theory of relativity no longer works. It can no more explain the properties of the *singularity* (this is the scientific term for the state of supercompressed matter in the center of the black hole) any more than it can explain what was happening during the very early stages of the evolution of the universe. In this case also, the long-sought theory of quantum gravity will be needed before we can attain a complete understanding.

FIG. 5: *Some black holes are bright. If a black hole is part of a binary star system, its intense gravity may draw matter from the surface of its companion star. If this happens, this matter will spiral into the black hole before it is absorbed. As it is, it will move faster and faster, and emit copious quantities of energy in the form of light and other radiation. Thus, although the black hole cannot be seen, its presence can be deduced.*

Scientists do know, however, that black holes live up to their name. They are perfectly black objects. Nothing that has fallen into a black hole can ever escape, not even light. Though black holes emit no light—or any other kind of radiation—they can nevertheless be detected. If a black hole is part of a binary star system, its intense gravity will draw matter from the surface of its companion. This matter will emit copious quantities of radiation as it is accelerated and spirals into the black hole. Once it disappears, it will never be seen again. We can only observe matter before the black hole gobbles it up.

Neutron stars and black holes are the remnants of very massive stars. The higher temperatures and pressures that exist in the cores of these stars cause them to undergo more violent deaths than that which will be experienced by our sun. As the core contracts and becomes hotter during the latter stages of the star's life, carbon and helium combine to form oxygen. As the temperature rises still more, heavier elements are produced until the star has a core of iron, the most stable element of all. The creation of elements heavier than iron does not produce energy; in order to form heavier elements, energy must be supplied.

When the star's nuclear fuel is finally exhausted, the core collapses. As it does, an explosion occurs that sends the outer layers of the star flying off into space. The reactions that take place are so violent that some elements heavier than iron are formed. But they are not created in great quantities. The fact that iron is the end product of energy-producing fusion is what makes that metal so much more common than heavier ones such as lead or gold or uranium.

There are actually two types of supernova. The kind that I have just described is called Type II. Type I supernovas are associated with white dwarfs that are members of binary systems. If the stars are close to one another, the dwarf may draw matter from the surface of the other star. Type I supernovas occur when a white dwarf gains enough mass to put it over the limit of 1.4 times the mass of the sun. When this happens, the electron degeneracy pressure can no longer hold up the star, and it collapses in a manner similar to that of a star that produces a Type II supernova. Type I supernovas can be distinguished from those of Type II because they are all equally bright, and because no hydrogen is seen when they explode. There is hydrogen in a Type II supernova because events take place so rapidly and violently that some of the star's hydrogen never has a chance to fuse into helium. Type I supernovas have produced most of the iron in the universe, while most of the other heavy elements are created in those of Type II. Both kinds play important roles in cosmic evolution.

Supernovas are seen very rarely. It is estimated that they occur at a rate of 1 per century per galaxy. However a century is a very short time compared to the age of the universe, and supernovas were more common in the past, simply because the rate of star formation was higher than it is now.[3] Thus there has been plenty of time for the heavier elements to be produced.

The material that is expelled in supernova explosions is incorporated into succeeding generations of stars and the planets that form around them. The elements of which we and our planet are made, such as carbon, oxygen, nitrogen, silicon, and iron would not exist if space had not been enriched with supernova remnants.

A lot of complicated reactions take place when a star becomes a supernova. But the process is well understood, at least in its broad outlines. Proof of the correctness of supernova theories came in 1987 when a supernova was observed in the Large Magellanic Cloud, a small galaxy that is a satellite of the Milky Way. It occurred in a star that was close enough to have been observed and cataloged, and the light that it emitted was observed by numerous astronomers. Cosmic rays[4] produced by the supernova were also seen and measured, as was radio energy emitted in the explosion.

But the most striking observation was the detection of a stream of neutrinos that was seen before the visible light produced by the explosion arrived. Scientists had long theorized that the collapse of the core in a supernova was associated by the release of energy in the form of neutrinos.

Neutrinos are light particles that are ubiquitous in the

universe. There are about 100 million of them for every proton, and they travel at nearly the speed of light. Countless numbers of them pass through our bodies every second. But this does no harm because they rarely interact with other matter. Most of the neutrinos that come our way pass through the entire earth unimpeded.

Nevertheless, neutrinos can be observed. Scientists use huge underground detectors that are capable of recording rare neutrino events. They are constructed underground to filter out the cosmic rays that might otherwise contaminate the experimental results. When the neutrinos that preceded the visible signs of the supernova explosion were observed, this only confirmed what scientists had long believed. However, it is always gratifying to have experimental proof.

This supernova explosion wasn't a large one. It was considerably less luminous than many Type II supernova that had been seen in other galaxies. But it provided scientists with a wealth of observational data, making it possible to understand the reactions that take place in such explosions better than ever.

THE FORMATION OF THE SOLAR SYSTEM

Five billion years ago our solar system began to condense from a cloud of interstellar gas and dust. The gas was mostly hydrogen and helium and the dust grains consisted of elements that had been formed in supernovas. This condensation could very well have been triggered by the shock wave from a nearby supernova explosion. Numerous stars are created that way today.

As the cloud collapsed, a dense, slowly rotating core was formed. This core was to become the sun. It was surrounded by a disk of dust and gas that was spinning more rapidly. The centrifugal forces created by this rapid motion kept it from falling into the sun.

Like the gas clouds that condensed into galaxies and

stars, the disk contained fluctuations in density. Regions that were denser than average exerted gravitational forces on their surroundings, and much of the dust came together into small clumps. Calculations indicate that they were about the size of asteroids, and they are called planetesimals. At this time, no planets yet existed.

Gravity caused the largest planetesimals to become more massive yet. Collisions between them caused large bodies to form from smaller ones. Scientists believe, for example, that the nascent earth was once struck by a large body that may have been the size of Mars. But, although many of these encounters were quite violent, the net effect was to cause the planetesimals to grow in size.

Gas as well as dust was attracted to the planetesimals. Planets such as Jupiter and Saturn, called gas giants because they are composed primarily of gas, have rocky cores. But the cores make up only a small part of the total volumes. The inner planets, on the other hand, were not large enough to retain much hydrogen or helium, light gasses that boiled off into space. A small planet does not exert gravitational forces that are strong enough to retain light elements.

The earth was formed 4.6 billion years ago. At that time, the planets experienced numerous collisions with asteroids. Studies of the moon, Mercury, and Mars indicate that impact craters were created then at a rate about a thousand times greater than they are today. And of course every time a planet experienced a collision, its mass increased. During the first 100 million years of the formation of the solar system, the planets increased in size to something close to what they have today.

The numerous bodies that the primordial earth collided with produced so much energy that the earth formed a molten core that was composed mostly of iron. The core is still liquid today. The energy released by the radioactive decay of elements within it keeps it hot. As the iron core formed, lighter elements floated to the surface, creating a rocky mantle. This too remained molten; the early earth had no solid surface.

At first, the earth's atmosphere probably consisted mainly of nitrogen and carbon dioxide. There was little or no oxygen. The oxygen in our atmosphere was created much later by photosynthesizing bacteria. There were no oceans either. Most of the water that is present on the earth's surface today was released from the mantle in volcanic eruptions. The water is believed to have come originally from collisions with comets, which are mostly ice (comets are sometimes described as "dirty ice balls"; the "dirt" consists of small amounts of various other substances).

It seems that one could not think of a more inhospitable environment for the creation of life. Not only was the earth extremely hot, it also received a great deal of ultraviolet radiation from the sun. Since there was no oxygen in the atmosphere, there was no ozone layer to shield the ultraviolet out.

Yet life evolved, and it evolved quickly. It seems to have appeared almost as soon as conditions became more favorable. That is the subject of the next chapter.

NOTES

[1] More specifically a proton, an electron, and an antineutrino. I am using the word neutrino here as a generic term. Neutrinos and antineutrinos have similar properties; and they would annihilate each other, producing a small burst of energy, if they happened to collide. However, this almost never happens; a neutrino of either variety is much more likely to interact with a proton or a neutron.

[2] Naturally occurring beryllium has a mass number of 9. It contains 4 protons and 5 neutrons. The presence of the extra neutron makes it stable.

[3] At this moment, new stars are being created in the spiral arms of our galaxy.

[4] Cosmic rays are not really a form of radiation. They consist of atomic nuclei that travel through space at high velocities.

CHAPTER 3

THE CREATION OF LIFE

The most amazing thing about our universe is the fact that the creation of life seems somehow to have been written into the laws of physics. This is a more remarkable thing than one might think. We seem to live in a very special kind of universe. If these laws were just slightly different than what they are, life could never have appeared. The universe would exist, but there would be no one to see it.

For example, if gravity were just slightly weaker than it is, stars and galaxies would never have formed. Gravity would not have been strong enough to cause the primordial hydrogen and helium gas to condense the way it has in our universe. If gravity were a little stronger, the gas would have condensed more rapidly. And when it did, the heat generated in stellar cores would have been so great that the nuclear fuel would have burned at a very rapid pace. An average size star like our sun would burn out rapidly, so rapidly that life would be extinguished quickly even if it somehow managed to evolve. And if gravity were strong enough, stars would explode like bombs shortly after they were created.

The neutron is slightly heavier than the proton. As a result, it can decay into a proton and an electron (and, of course, a neutrino). This reaction does not take place because the neutron is a composite particle. It isn't; the electron is spontaneously created in the reaction. But if the reverse were the case, if protons were heavier, then they would decay into neutrons, and there would be no atoms. After all, an electron will not attach itself to a particle that has no electrical charge. In such a case, space would be filled with nothing but neutrons. And if the forces that bind particles together in atomic nuclei were 5 percent weaker than they are, deuterium could not be formed. The forces would not be strong enough to bind a proton and a neutron together. If deuterium did not exist, no element heavier than hydrogen could be formed. The creation of deuterium is the first step in nucleosynthesis. If bodies the size of stars did form, they would never ignite, And of course it is difficult to imagine living organisms that were made of nothing but cold hydrogen gas.

If the electromagnetic force that binds molecules together was a little weaker, solids and liquids could not be created. If this force was a little stronger, no nucleus containing more than one proton could exist. The electrical repulsion between positively charged protons would prevent this. Again, there would be nothing in the universe but hydrogen.

As we have seen, elements heavier than lithium were not created in the big bang; they can be formed only in the cores of stars. The creation of these elements seems to depend upon a fortuitous coincidence. Quantum mechanics tells us that an atomic nucleus can possess only certain definite amounts of energy. It can be in one energy state or another; it cannot posses a quantity of energy that falls between them. Now it so happens that the beryllium and carbon nuclei have energy levels that are in just the right places to allow carbon to be formed. If these levels were a little higher or lower, only the elements synthesized in the big bang would exist. Interestingly, the existence of the relevant energy level of the carbon nucleus was suggested by Fred Hoyle before it was found by nuclear physicists. When the physicists, who didn't appreciate having an astronomer telling them about their specialty, finally began to look for the level, they found it to be exactly what Hoyle had said it must be.

It is almost as though the universe had been consciously designed to allow for the emergence of life. I say *almost* because this fact doesn't necessarily imply the existence of a Creator. Many scientists believe that there are countless other universes, perhaps an infinite number of them. If the laws are not always the same, then the vast majority of them are lifeless. Our universe is the way it is because if it were not, we would not be here to see it.[1]

I'll have more to say about the subject of an infinity of universes in the last chapter of this part when I give a brief account of some current cosmological speculation. But for now, I will continue to confine myself to discussing facts that can either be observed, or deduced from what has been observed, and jump right into discussion of the creation of life. I make no excuses for shifting suddenly from cosmology and astrophysics to biology. The creation of life is part of cosmic evolution too.

THE ORIGIN OF LIFE

Life appears to have evolved on the earth with extraordinary rapidity. Impacts with asteroids and meteorites early in the earth's history released so much heat that the earth's surface remained molten for as long as 800 million years. Since the earth has existed for about 4.6 billion years, this means that it lacked a solid surface until about 3.8 billion years ago. Yet a billion years after the earth was created it was teeming with life. Fossils of organisms resembling blue-green algae have been found in rocks in Australia and Africa that have an age of 3.5 billion years. And chemical traces of life have been found in rocks in Greenland that have an age of 3.85 billion years. If there really were living organisms at that early a date, they are not necessarily our ancestors. They might have been wiped out by an impact with some large extraterrestrial body, and life could have evolved again later. In any case, life seems to have evolved as soon as the earth's crust cooled enough for oceans to form, creating a hospitable environment.

Scientists believe that the ingredients for the creation of life were present at the time that the crust cooled. Many organic chemicals have been detected in space, including amino acids, the building blocks from which proteins are formed. When a cloud of gas becomes cool enough, chemical reactions will take place. In fact, some of the molecular clouds that have been found in space contain enough ethyl alcohol to give a party for the population of the entire galaxy.

However, it was amino acids—not alcohol—that played a fundamental role in the evolution of life. They might have been carried to the earth's surface on falling interplanetary dust particles, or they could equally well have come from the tails of comets that brushed the earth's atmosphere. Most likely, both processes took place. Amino acids could also have been created on the earth itself. Numerous experiments have been performed that have shown that this is possible. Scientists are not entirely sure about the composition of the atmosphere of the primordial earth, although most think that carbon dioxide and nitrogen were present in the largest quantities. However, experiments have been performed in various different kinds of simulated atmosphere, and it has been shown that amino acids and nucleotides—the components of DNA—can be created under a variety of different conditions.

Amino acids and the other chemicals necessary to life will not form if oxygen is present. However, photosynthesizing organisms began to release large quantities of oxygen into the atmosphere only 2 billion years ago. Thus the conditions for the creation of life seem to have been ideal.

Living organisms didn't begin to colonize the land until a little over 400 million years ago; the first land plants appeared at that time. For 3 billion years life existed only in the oceans. However, we can be reasonably sure that it did not originate there. Amino acids and other organic chemicals were present in the primordial oceans only in small quantities. As a result, the reactions that created more complex molecules could not have taken place very often. Furthermore, water acts to break chains of amino acids apart. If any proteins had formed in the oceans 3.5 billion years ago, they would have disintegrated almost immediately.

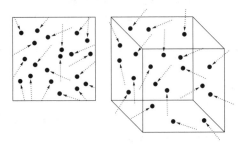

FIG. 6: *Concentrating organic molecules on a surface. If a solution of organic chemicals is concentrated on a surface (FIG. 6A), then they are more likely to encounter one another than if they are in a three-dimensional volume (FIG. 6B). It is easier to "miss" another molecule in three dimensions than in two.*

However, there were other environments in which life could have originated more readily. If the heat of the sun caused the water in a tide pool to evaporate, the solution of organic chemicals that it contained would have become more concentrated. Under such conditions, the chemicals would meet up with one another more frequently, and reactions between them would proceed much more rapidly. Life may very well have originated, as Darwin suggested, in some "warm little pond." According to another, currently very popular, theory, the chemical evolution that led to life took place on clay surfaces. If chemicals adhere to a two-dimensional surface, they will encounter one another more often than they will in a three-dimensional pool. One of the things that makes chess so complicated a game is the fact that it is two-, not three-dimensional. The pieces can interact with one another in a myriad of different ways.

[46]

Scientists are not sure about the conditions under which life began. However, they all agree that some kind of chemical evolution must have preceded the creation of life. Under the right conditions, progressively more complex organic molecules can form. But did life begin with proteins, or with RNA (a simpler relative of DNA)? No one knows. Both are essential to life. But there seems to be no way to tell which came first. Scientists can only agree that it seems unlikely that the first life was not based on DNA. All living organisms today make use of DNA as a carrier of their genetic code. But DNA is made up of two intertwined strands (the *double helix*). Proteins are required if these strands are to be separated from one another so that the DNA can reproduce. But the DNA must first be split apart if proteins are to be manufactured. DNA by itself is relatively inert.

The "life began with proteins" theory and the "RNA first" hypothesis are not the only possibilities. An interesting theory has been put forward by Stuart Kauffman, a theoretical biologist at the Santa Fe Institute in New Mexico. Kauffman has performed computer simulations that seem to indicate that life will spring into existence spontaneously when a set of organic chemicals attains a certain degree of complexity. According to Kauffman's theory, it doesn't matter whether RNA or proteins evolved first; the complexity of the interactions between chemicals is the important thing. Many scientists find this to be a very appealing idea. But unfortunately, there seems to be no obvious way to test Kauffman's theory experimentally.

But at least it is possible to describe the origin of life in broad outlines. Organic chemicals were present on the primordial earth. Under the right conditions, they were able to react with one another to form more complex chemicals. Eventually chemical systems that could reproduce themselves were created. If the systems could also mutate, they were, in effect, simple living organisms. Evolution continued, and the earth's oceans were soon full of primitive algae and bacteria. Finally, over a period of billions of years, these evolved into the life forms that populate the earth today.

LIFE IN THE UNIVERSE

The fact that life arose so quickly on Earth leads scientists to believe that it is probably ubiquitous in the universe. The discovery of planets in other star systems has strengthened this belief, since it seems to confirm the idea that a great number of stars have planets. Scientists are especially interested in the possibility that there might have been life on Mars. Today, Mars has very little atmosphere, and there is virtually no water. However, there are indications that water flowed on its surface in the distant past, and it is believed that Mars once had an atmosphere that has since leaked off into space. Mars is a small planet and its relatively weak gravity would not retain atmospheric gasses as readily as that of the earth has.

Naturally no one thinks that we will discover that Mars was once populated by little green men. If life once existed there, then there was probably not enough time for complex organisms to evolve. However, we might very well discover traces of micro-organisms on its surface. Incidentally, contrary to what some scientists initially believed, the Martian meteorite that received so much attention in the media during the late 1990s probably does not contain traces of life. During the years after its discovery, the evidence of life that it contained began to seem less and less conclusive, and the current scientific consensus is that the meteorite contains nothing but inorganic forms.

Until some kind of extraterrestrial life is discovered, however, we cannot be sure that life is common in the universe. Life did arise quickly on Earth, but we cannot be entirely certain that it did not happen by chance. For all we know, the existence of life may depend on some very improbable chemical events, and earth may be the only planet with life in our galaxy. The fact that scientists have not determined exactly how life originated introduces an element of uncertainty, one that may never go away. After all, we can't go back 3.5 or 3.8 billion years to observe the earliest life. All that scientists can do is invent plausible scenarios. Under these circumstances, there is no way of knowing for sure whether life is a very rare or a very common thing.

Suppose, for example, that life first evolved in tide pools. This could never have happened if the earth did not have a large moon that exerts tidal forces. But how common are large moons such as ours? No one is sure. We know only that earth is the only one of the inner planets that has one. Venus and Mercury have no moons, and the moons of Mars are quite small, too small to have any influence on events that take place on the surface of that planet. On the other hand, if life evolved on clay surfaces, it is probably relatively common. After all there is nothing very unique about the chemical makeup of the substances found on the earth's surface. Most likely they exist on many earthlike planets. If ideas about nucleosynthesis are correct—and we can be reasonably sure that they are—then there must be many planets with chemical makeups similar to that of the earth. But as long as we are ignorant about the precise mechanisms that were involved, we can't be certain that life on earth does not depend upon environmental conditions that were special in some way.

However, the idea that the universe is full of life certainly seems very plausible. So it is worthwhile to speculate about what extraterrestrial life might be like. When we do this, we are again confronted with a series of uncertainties. For example, it took over 3 billion years for multicellular life forms to evolve on earth. Fossil evidence indicates that they first began to evolve during the last phases of the geological period called the Precambian, some 680 to 570 million years ago. We have no way of knowing whether this transition was inevitable, or whether certain special conditions were required. It may very well be that most life never progresses beyond this stage. There will be no way that we can be sure until we attain a better understanding of the mechanisms that caused life to evolve the way it has.

It is this fact, incidentally, that makes the search for life on Mars so important. If we did find life, or evidence of past life, on that planet, many of these doubts would be removed. Then we could indeed say with confidence that we live in a universe that is probably full of living organisms. Scientists might even be able to make some inferences about the origin of multicellular organisms.

EXTRATERRESTRIAL CIVILIZATIONS

Let us assume that life has indeed evolved in many different places. In spite of all the various gaps in our knowledge, this idea seems very plausible. What, then, is the chance that we might eventually encounter another advanced technological civilization? Are attempts to communicate with them by looking for radio signals that might be coming to us through interstellar space really worthwhile?

We might as well begin by assuming that multicellular life is an inevitable consequence of evolution. After all, it seems a very natural thing. Many single-celled organisms form colonies, and there is every reason to suspect that, over time, evolution would cause multicellular life to emerge. Intermediate forms do exist on earth. For example, the jellyfish known as the Portuguese man-of-war looks like a single organism. But it is really a colony of individuals that have taken on specialized functions. The float, the tentacles, the reproductive organs, and the parts of the man-of-war that digest food all have the same genetic makeup. However, the man-of-war is a colony, not a multi-cellular organism. The various individual organisms of which it is composed have assumed different forms. It is not difficult to imagine that the man-of-war represents a stage in the evolution of true multicellularity.

On the other hand, the evolution of intelligence is a more problematical matter, and we have no way of knowing how likely it is. After all, intelligence evolved only once on earth, and it could conceivably be quite rare elsewhere in the universe. Evolution, after all, does not progress toward any goals. It depends upon the workings of blind chance. In doing so, it creates organisms that are well adapted to their environments. But it would be absurd to maintain that our intelligence necessarily makes us better adapted than other creatures. The genus homo has been around only for something like 2 million years. We are nowhere near matching the success of the cockroach, which evolved some 300 million years ago. Its adaptation is superb. There was something about life on the African savannah that caused our ancestors to evolve big brains. But we don't really know what this something was, or how common it might be elsewhere in the universe. If the evolution of intelligence was an easy transition, it would have occurred in some dinosaur species. After all, the dinosaurs existed for a considerably longer time than we have. But, for some reason, intelligence didn't evolve then. True, some dinosaurs were getting reasonably smart by the time that they were wiped out by an impact with an asteroid. But they might never have "progressed" any further.

If intelligence does evolve, there is no guarantee that a technological civilization will develop. Again, this is something that has happened only once on earth. There have been numerous advanced civilizations on earth. They developed in Greece, in China and India, in the new world, and in other locations. The Mayans, to cite just one example, had quite a complex society. But experimental science developed only in western Europe. It is true that science and technology are not quite the same thing. In fact, many of the technological innovations in western civilization were made before there was any science to explain them. However, science is necessary if a civilization is to develop the very sophisticated devices that are so common today. The craft of sword making reached impressive heights long before scientists understood anything about the properties of alloys. But technological craftsmanship alone could never have produced the modern electronic computer.

So it is entirely possible that there exist intelligent species in the universe that never develop technologies. We just don't know. However, the cost of looking for radio signals from other civilizations is minimal compared to the probable benefits. We can't even imagine what we might learn if we gained access to even a part of the knowledge gained by another intelligent species.

Contact is likely to be a matter of radio transmissions, by the way. There is every reason to believe that extraterrestrial travel will never be feasible. The distance between star systems is huge. The nearest, the triple star system known as Alpha Centauri (which is not very likely to harbor life), is over 25 trillion miles away. It can be calculated that to travel to a nearby star in some reasonable period of time would require an expenditure of energy greater than the energy production of our world over a period of a century. This calculation does not depend upon any assumptions about the methods used. The development of as-yet-unknown technologies will not change the energy requirements. Attaining velocities approaching that of light would still be necessary, and this will never be cheap.

I am not implying that humanity will never spread beyond the solar system, only that interstellar voyages will likely always be impractical. Physicist Freeman Dyson, for example, has suggested that we might eventually colonize the comets, and that these might provide a springboard for venturing even farther into space. This is not an implausible idea. But if this ever happens, contact between the home planet and its frontiers is likely to remain a matter of radio contact only.

THE FUTURE OF LIFE

I will discuss the future evolution of the universe in the next chapter. However, this seems to be the proper place to talk about the future of life. I am not thinking about the ways in which life might evolve. Evolution may even have come to a halt in the human species. We have become so adept at controlling our environment that we are no longer subject to the evolutionary pressure to which other animals must adapt. In any case, if we do evolve further, there is no reason to think that it will necessarily be in the direction of greater intelligence. Evolution cannot be equated with progress, and there are no goals that it seeks to reach. In any case, human brain size appears to have reached a natural limit. Babies' large heads make birth very difficult in our species, and any further increase would only cause a greater incidence of mortality in both mothers and infants. This would hardly be a desirable evolutionary characteristic.

What, then, are the prospects for life in our universe? Well, nothing lasts forever, and life is not likely to be an exception. As the universe grows older, the energy sources that are available to us now will gradually fade away. Stars will burn out and become white dwarfs, or collapse as black holes. Radioactive elements will decay into stable ones. The heat that is currently present in the cores of planets will dissipate, and the universe will become a cold, dark place.

The energy that is present now will not disappear. Matter and energy are always conserved except when one is converted into the other. One form of energy can be changed into another; the production of heat by friction is just one example. However, life does not depend on the total amount of energy that is present, it depends on energy differences.

In order to see why this should be so, consider the production of hydroelectric power. This does not depend upon the total amount of energy that is available. There is a lot of gravitational energy in a mountain lake. But if the water does not fall from one level to another, no power can be produced. Similarly, no one has ever constructed a ship that will be powered by the heat energy present in the earth's oceans. Although a great deal of heat energy is present (every substance that is not at a temperature of absolute zero contains heat energy), it cannot be used.

When the sun become a white dwarf, the earth—if it still exists—will not be a place where hydroelectric power can be generated. The oceans will be frozen then. But even if they were not, the dim glow of the dying sun would not be sufficient to cause water to evaporate from the seas and to fall on land as rain. Similarly, the flow of energy from the sun to the earth will not be sufficient to maintain any kind of life. At present it is this flow that sustains us. Plants convert the energy in sunlight into foodstuffs that we can eat. We extract energy from them, and expel energy into our environment in different forms. In this sense, we are not unlike hydroelectric power stations.

The disappearance of usable energy in the universe is called *increasing entropy*. I have so far avoided using this term because it is often said that entropy is associated with increasing *disorder*. Although this interpretation is correct, I think that saying that energy differences will vanish gives a more intuitive picture of what will be happening. This is a correct interpretation of the law of entropy too. Instead of speaking of increasing disorder, it is possible to talk of the disappearance of energy differences. Mathematically they are the same thing.

There is no way that even a highly advanced civilization will be able to escape the *heat death* of the universe. Energy sources will eventually become so scarce that even the most advanced technology will not be able to extract usable energy from them. Nuclear fusion will certainly not be an answer. Over time, atomic nuclei that can be used to produce energy will evolve into inert elements such as iron, or be swallowed into black holes. And of course energy will be required to break heavy elements apart into the lighter ones that are necessary to life.

We can't be entirely certain how terminally serious the *heat death* of the universe will become. It may be that our universe will come to an end before the last vestiges of life disappear. As we shall see in the next chapter, it has sometimes been thought that there is a chance our universe may eventually begin to contract and finally collapse in a *big crunch* analogous to the big bang. I suspect, however, that if this does happen, many billion years will have passed since there were any sentient beings around to witness the proceedings.

Some people find this prospect rather depressing, even though the events that I have described will take place many billions of years after they are dead. However, it does not necessarily follow that life is destined to disappear forever. As I will briefly explain in Chapter 5 of this part, cosmologists often speculate about the possibility that new universes are created all the time. And if they are, naturally some of them may evolve life.

NOTES

[1] Naturally this doesn't disprove the existence of a Creator either. But I will say no more about this particular subject since it is a matter outside of science.

CHAPTER 4
THE FATE OF THE UNIVERSE

The universe is expanding. Meanwhile, gravity is slowing the expansion down. The gravitational attraction between galaxies and other mass in the universe produces a kind of braking action. Thus it seems natural to ask the question, Will the universe expand forever, or will gravity eventually cause the expansion to reverse, and a phase of contraction to begin?

As we shall see later, there may be some added complications. It has recently been discovered that the expansion of the universe may not depend upon the workings of gravity alone. However, there is nothing wrong with considering the simplest possible case first. In fact, this is the way that scientists generally approach a problem. They try to understand the main features of a phenomenon. Only after they have done that do they consider the effects of any complications that might be present. For example, if astronomers want to determine the path that will be followed by a comet, they first calculate the effects of the gravitational attraction of the sun. Only after they have done that do they consider the ways in which the various planets might perturb the comit's orbit.

According to Einstein's general theory of relativity, the universe may be either open or closed. An open universe is infinite in extent, and its expansion never stops. Gravity may slow the expansion down, but an open universe will expand for all eternity. A closed univese, on the other hand, is finite, and it will eventually collapse in a big crunch. The retarding effects of gravity in a closed universe are great enough that it must eventually begin to contract.

A closed universe has no boundaries, and there is nothing that *encloses it*. Gravity causes space to close in upon itself, and the geometry of a closed universe is a three-dimensional analogue of the two-dimensional surface of the earth. One can no more reach the *edge* of a closed universe than one can come to the ends of the earth. Of course there is a significant difference. The earth's surface is curved in three-dimensional space, but there is no fourth spatial dimension that a closed universe can be *curved in*. If you have trouble visualizing such a situation, you shouldn't be bothered. Physicists can't visualize it either. They have the same kinds of visual experience that you do, and form the same kinds of mental pictures. However, they realize that the equations of general relativity allow a universe of this form.

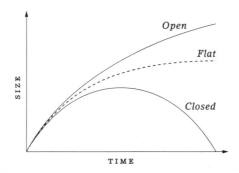

FIG. 7: *Open, closed, and flat universes. The diagram pictures the expansion (or ultimate contraction) of various different kinds of theoretical universes over periods of many billions of year. The expansion of a closed universe would eventually halt, and a phase of contraction would begin. An open universe would expand forever. In a flat universe, the expansion would continually slow down but never come to a complete halt. It is suspected that our universe is probably open.*

It is possible to circumnavigate the earth. Anyone who travels in any chosen direction, and never deviates from it, will eventually reach his starting point from the opposite direction. This is not possible in a closed universe, not even in theory, because such a universe does not last long enough for the journey to be completed. A ray of light that was emitted at the beginning of the big bang would reach its starting point at the moment the universe completed its collapse. Anything that traveled more slowly, or had a later start, could never complete the circuit.

There is actually a third kind of possible universe, one in which the geometry is *flat*. A flat universe is one that would be exactly on the borderline between open and closed. In a flat universe the rate of expansion approaches zero but never actually gets there. Like an open universe, it is infinite. But for all practical purposes we can discount this possibility. It represents only one out of an infinite number of different possibilities, and its probability is thus equal to zero.

Is our universe open or closed? No one knows for sure. It depends upon the density of matter in the universe, a quantity that cannot be measured with any great accuracy. The critical density is equal to about three hydrogen atoms per cubic meter. If the universe has a density that is greater than this, it is closed and will eventually collapse. If the density is less, the universe is open and will always expand. This is a consequence of the fact that, the higher the matter density of the universe, the stronger the gravitational retarding forces will be. Matter does not have to be compressed into stars and galaxies to exert gravitational force. Every hydrogen or helium nucleus contributes too. Naturally the gravity of a single nucleus is so small that no one will ever be able to devise a way to measure it. However, if there are enough nuclei, then their contribution to total gravitational force can be significant. Even tenuous intergalactic gas plays a role in slowing the expansion of the universe. Subatomic particles that moved through the universe randomly would have the same effect if there were enough of them.

DARK MATTER

It is easy to determine how much luminous matter there is in the universe. Since stellar evolution is well understood, astronomers need only measure the quantity of light that is emitted by a galaxy in order to estimate the quantity of matter that is present in stars and in glowing clouds of gas. Unfortunately, this does not provide scientists with a good estimate of the total amount of matter in the universe. It has been known since 1932 that the universe contains matter that astronomers cannot see. During the early 1930s the Dutch astronomer Jan Oort observed the motions of certain stars in our galaxy. He concluded that these motions could not be explained if it was assumed that the visible matter was the only mass present. In 1933, the year after Oort published his results, the California Institute of Technology astronomer Fritz Zwicky observed a large cluster of galaxies in the constellation Coma Berenices. He noted that the galaxies in the cluster seemed to be held together by their mutual gravitational attraction, even though the mass that was present in the galaxies' stars was only a fraction of the quantity that was needed.

Today, astronomers know that at least 90 percent, and perhaps as much as 99 percent, of the mass of the universe exists in the form of dark matter (*invisible matter* might be a more descriptive term; dark matter is matter that astronomers cannot see, not a material that is dark in color). Since no one knows how much dark matter there is, it is impossible to calculate whether the universe is open, closed, or near the borderline. Most are of the opinion that the universe is open; the matter present in stars is only about 1 percent of that which would produce a closed universe. But there is no way to calculate the total mass density.[1]

Some of the dark matter consists of black holes, white dwarfs, and brown dwarfs. Although white dwarfs are not dark, they are so dim that they cannot be seen if they are too far away. At least some of the dark matter is surely made up of subatomic particles. If there are enough of them in the universe, they would exert gravitational forces far greater than that of the stars and galaxies.

It is thought that some of the dark matter is made up of neutrinos. The neutrino, whose existence was postulated by the Austrian physicist Wolfgang Pauli in 1931 and detected experimentally in 1956, was originally presumed to be a particle of zero mass that traveled at the velocity of light. During the early 1980s, physicists began to wonder if the neutrino might not actually have a small but finite mass, one that could somehow be detected. This idea was confirmed in 1998 when experiments performed in Japan confirmed that it was not massless. The experiments didn't measure the neutrino mass directly, only the mass difference between two different kinds (there are three distinct varieties of neutrino). However, the mass of the neutrino is probably something of the order of 100,000 times smaller than that of an electron. And the electron itself is a light particle; it weighs almost 2000 times less than a proton or a neutron. However, since there are about 100 milion neutrinos for every proton or electron, their contribution to the total mass of the universe could be significant.

The neutrino cannot be the only significant component of dark matter in the universe. Any dark matter that was present in the early universe would have influenced galaxy formation, and calculations indicate that galaxies and clusters of galaxies would not have formed—or would not have assumed the forms that astronomers see—if only neutrinos and the primordial hydrogen and helium gas had been present. Thus most cosmologists believe that some of the dark matter consists of other kinds of particles, possibly ones that have not yet been discovered.

It is possible to sum all this up by saying that scientists do not know whether our universe has a mass density that is greater than, or less than, the critical value because they don't really know what the universe is made of. Stars, galaxies, and interstellar and intergalactic gas can make up only a small part of the whole. All that observations can tell us is that the mass density is probably somewhere between one-tenth and ten times the critical value. As I write this, the lower values seem somewhat more likely.

If the inflationary universe theory is true, the density is probably so close to the borderline that we will never be able to tell the difference. If there was a rapid, inflationary expansion when the universe was much less than one second old, this would have had the effect of "flattening out" the space in which we live. This effect can be seen when a balloon is blown up. As the balloon expands, its surface becomes flatter and flatter. Similarly, the surface of the earth seems flat to the naked eye; the curvature of the earth is too small to be noticed under most circumstances. On the other hand, if you stood on a small asteroid, the curvature of its surface would be very obvious.

However, one can't say with confidence that the universe is very nearly flat. This conclusion is based on theory only, and theories are frequently modified. I, for one, would be very surprised if it were eventually proved that an inflationary expansion did not take place. But I wouldn't be surprised at all if it were discovered that this expansion did not happen exactly the way that scientists think.

THE UNIVERSE IN THE DISTANT FUTURE

If the universe is closed, it will eventually begin to contract. It is not likely that there will be any sentient creatures around to observe this event. It will take place 50 billion or more years in the future. By that time, most of the stars will have burned out; the universe will contain only small, very dim stars, black holes, and white and black dwarfs. Stars are still being created now, but the supply of interstellar gas from which they are formed is rapidly becoming exhausted. At present, the rate of star formation is a hundred or more times smaller than it was when the universe was young. Of course an advanced technological civilization might find ways to survive for a very long time. But 50 billion years (and the actual figure could be much greater than that) is a very, very long time.

If a big crunch took place, the universe would eventually contract to an almost infinitesimally small volume and be crushed out of existence. At one time, scientists engaged in a lot of speculation about the possibility that it might experience a *bounce*, and begin to expand again in a new big bang. But the more closely they examined this idea, the more unlikely it seemed. One of the major stumbling blocks was the realization that the entropy, or disorder, in a universe that recycled itself in this manner would increase from cycle to cycle. After one or two bounces we would have a universe that could not possibly sustain life. Another problem associated with the idea of a bouncing universe is the fact that starlight would presumably accumulate from cycle to cycle. Thus, if the universe bounced in the past, we should be surrounded by starlight from previous cycles. Of course, no one is absolutely certain about what the fate of a closed universe will be. However, if there eventually is a big crunch, it is probably safe to assume that it will be the end.

FIG. 8: *The expansion of the universe. As the universe expands, it becomes progressively "flatter." This is analogous to the blowing up of a balloon. As the balloon expands, its surface becomes less curved. If the inflationary universe theory is correct, then an early, massive expansion would have "pushed" the universe into a state very close to the borderline between open and closed.*

If the universe is open, then the expansion will continue relentlessly. The stars will eventually burn out and become black dwarfs or black holes. Matter itself may endure over long periods of time. For example, the electron and the proton are the most stable particles known. No one has ever seen a proton decay. However, according to some theories, such decays do eventually take place. Over periods of time much longer than the present age of the universe, the proton may disintegrate into lighter particles, including positrons (positively charged electrons). When an electron and a positron encounter one another, they undergo mutual anihilation, and a gamma ray will be created in their place. If this happens, the gamma rays will eventually be degraded into low-energy radiation, just as the light that was emitted in the big bang has been transformed into microwaves. Thus, an open universe will eventually become a cold, dark place, containing nothing but a few light particles and some diffuse radiation. Even the black holes that it contains may not last forever. According to a theory proposed by the British physicist Stephen Hawking, black holes eventually evaporate into streams of particles. If this happens, the fate of these particles would be the same as those that make up ordinary matter.

Stars do not last forever. Nor do galaxies, for that matter. We haven't seen any galaxies break up yet. But over periods of many billions of years, random motions should cause some stars to be ejected into intergalactic space, while others will condense into the enormous black holes that are often found in galactic cores. There exists strong evidence that many galaxies, including our own, have black holes in their centers. These supermassive black holes have masses that are hundreds of thousands or millions of times greater than that of our sun.

We know that life must eventually come to and end, and that a similar fate will befall the stars and galaxies. There is no reason to doubt that the universe itself will eventually die.

But of course this might not be the end. As we will see in the final chapter, there is currently a great deal of speculation (which is not supported by any empirical evidence, however) to the effect that new universes may spring into existence all the time. If they do, there should be universes very much like ours, and forms of intelligent life very much like us. The idea of cosmic cycles that is encountered in so many different mythologies may contain some truth after all.

EINSTEIN'S "BLUNDER"

Shortly after he published his general theory of relativity in 1915, Einstein began looking for solutions to his equations that would describe the state of the universe. He found, to his surprise, that the simplest possible solutions implied that the universe had either to be expanding or contracting. Now, at the time, no one had ever suggested that the universe was not stable. It had been believed since the time of Aristotle that it was unchanging. In fact, in 1915, many astronomers believed that our Milky Way galaxy *was* the universe. It had not yet been established that certain *nebula* (as they were called then) lay outside it.

Therefore Einstein added a term to his equations that he called the *cosmological constant*. This constant represented a repulsive force that would balance out the effects of gravity at great distances. But this turned out to be a mistake. Other scientists soon discovered that Einstein's universe would not be stable under any conditions. Even with the cosmological constant added in, the slightest perturbation would send it into a state of expansion or contraction. Einstein's universe was like a pencil balanced on its point, ready to fall in one direction or another. At first Einstein wouldn't accept these findings, and suggested that the mathematics used to derive them must contain some mistake. But he finally had to admit that he was the one who had been wrong. In fact, if he had not introduced the constant, he could have shown that the universe must be expanding. As it was, the world had to wait until the American astronomer Edwin Hubble performed observations that demonstrated the expansion of the universe in 1929.

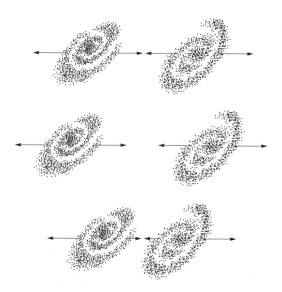

FIG. 9: *Einstein's balanced universe. Einstein originally conceived of the universe as static. In his view, the mutual gravitational attraction of the galaxies was balanced by an outward force. In* FIG. 9A, *two galaxies are shown, and the inward and outward forces are represented by arrows of the same length. However, it was soon shown that Einstein's universe would not be static after all. If galaxies happened to move just slightly farther apart (*FIG. 9B*), the gravitational attraction would decrease while the outward force remained the same. This would lead to continued expansion. If, on the other hand, galaxies happened to move just slightly closer together, the inward force would increase (*FIG. 9C*), and the universe would contract. Einstein's universe, in other words, would be unstable. Einstein later called this conception the greatest blunder of his life.*

Einstein was later to describe the introduction of the cosmological constant as his "greatest blunder," and a number of writers, myself included (I may possibly have been the first) have referred to it as a "fudge factor." But this characterization is really somewhat unfair. The most general solutions of the equations of general relativity do include a cosmological constant, and there is no a priori reason to think that it should be zero. Furthermore, Einstein had no reason to consider the possibility of an expanding universe. After all, the idea was unknown at the time.

In the decades that followed, astronomers were able to establish that, if there were a cosmological constant, it was too small to be measured. No repulsive forces were found. Nor did there seem to be any attractive forces other than gravity (the cosmological constant would give rise to an attractive force if it were negative).

But then, in 1998, all this suddenly changed. In January of that year, Saul Perlmutter of Lawrence Berkeley National Laboratory announced that he and a team of international observers had studied a total of forty distant supernovas. They had found that, not only had the expansion rate of the universe slowed too little for gravity ever to bring it to a stop, they had also found evidence of a previously unknown repulsive force. According to team member Alexei Fillipenko of the University of California at Berkeley, there was actually evidence that the expansion was speeding up. Einstein's cosmological constant, these scientists concluded, might indeed represent something very real.

In order to understand how they obtained this result, you only need to remember two things. First, when astronomers look very far out into space, they are also looking back in time. A galaxy or a supernova that is 10 billion light years away is observed as it was 10 billion years in the past. Also, all Type I supernova are of the same brightness. Recall that a Type I supernova explosion occurs when a white dwarf draws material from a nearby companion star. When the dwarf's mass increases to a certain point, it explodes like a bomb. Actually, all Type I supernova do not have exactly the same brightness. Those that fade more quickly are less luminous. But the variations are not great, and they can be corrected for. It is thus possible to tell how far away a Type I supernova is.

The same method could be used to measure the distance of, say, a 100-watt light bulb. A bulb that is nearby will seem very bright, where one that is far away would appear to be a dim speck. It would only be necessary to measure the light coming from the bulb to determine its distance. In practice, no one would do this. It would be much simpler to measure the distance with a tape measure. However, a tape measure cannot be laid out in space, so the apparent brightness method is often used to calculate precisely how far away distant objects are.

When the light coming from the Type I supernovas was measured, it was found that, on the average, the most distant ones were 10 to 15 percent farther away than they would be in a universe in which the expansion had slowed very little or not at all. The expansion of the universe had carried them to greater distances than astronomers had previously thought.

Of course the findings were not totally conclusive. It is conceivable that the earliest stars, which formed some 10 to 12 billion years ago were different from present-day stars in some unknown way, and that the Type I supernovas that they produced differed in brightness from more recent ones. However, this possibility is not very likely, and as I write this, no one has come up with a theory to explain how this could be the case. Robert Kirshner of the Harvard-Smithsonian Center for Astrophysics has suggested that there could be some "sneaky little effect" that is skewing the results. But no one has made any suggestions as to what this sneaky little effect could be.

Comments like Kirshner's aren't just carping. This is the kind of thing that goes on every time a new scientific discovery is made. Scientists always try to think up alternative explanations for a newly discovered phenomenon, and if none of these prove to be viable, then they conclude that the discovery is real. As I write this, no one has put forward any very good ideas, however. The fact that scientists such as Kirshner can only suggest some "sneaky little effect" is indicative of this. Thus it appears that it is necessary to at least tentatively accept the conclusion that something is causing the expansion of the universe to accelerate. This is tantamount to saying that a cosmological constant exists; the constant is nothing more than a mathematical way of expressing the fact that the expansion of the universe depends on something besides gravity.

Some scientists, such as University of Chicago cosmologist Michael Turner, suggest that the discovery indicates that the universe contains some form of energy that we don't understand. However, there have so far not been any very good ideas as to what this energy might be. Attempts to explain an accelerating acceleration theoretically have—again, as I write this—succeeded only in generating controversy. For example, Stephen Hawking and his Cambridge University colleague Neil Turok have come up with a mathematical explanation of how the universe could transform itself into an eternally expanding one. But other cosmologists, such as Andrei Linde of Stanford University, are skeptical. As Linde points out, the approach of Hawking and Turok describes many possible universes, most of which contain no matter. "This prediction," he says, "tells us that we must practically live in an empty universe, which disagrees with observations."

It is not likely that the matter will be settled until further observations are made. Observations of the pattern of fluctuations in the cosmic microwave background may provide a clue. As I write this, two such experiments are planned. Both will probe the background from satellites, and the later of the two will not be launched until 2006. It appears that the discoveries that will be made in cosmology in the years ahead are likely to be exciting indeed. Our understanding of the universe might very well be transformed in significant ways.

At the moment, it is possible to form one conclusion. Whatever the cause of the accelerating expansion might be (if it is indeed real), we have one more piece of evidence to indicate that we live in an open universe, one that will expand forever.

NOTES

[1] If the inflationary universe theory is correct, then the universe should be so close to the borderline that we will never be able to determine whether the mass density is just slightly above or just slightly below the critical value. However, though the idea that there was a period of inflationary expansion early in the history of the universe is appealing, interesting, and widely accepted, there is really no observational evidence to support the theory. As the British biologist T.H. Huxley, an early supporter of Darwin, once noted, there have been many beautiful theories that were eventually refuted by *ugly facts*. It is not inconceivable that the inflationary universe theory could experience the same fate.

CHAPTER 5
UNIVERSES WITHOUT END, OR THE COSMOS IS A BIG NOTHING

The big bang theory was originally proposed in 1927 by the Belgian astronomer and Roman Catholic priest Georges Lemaître. Lemaître suggested that if one extrapolated back in time, a picture of galaxies growing closer and closer together would result. Originally, according to his theory, all of the matter in the universe was crushed together in a kind of *cosmic egg* or *primeval atom*. The big bang consisted of an explosion of this *egg*. When George Gamow elaborated upon Lemaître's ideas in the 1940s, he retained this concept, but called the primordial material *ylem*.

It is difficult to conceive of all the matter in the universe as having been condensed into a minute volume, even though we know that something similar happens at the center of a black hole, where all of the matter that remains of a dead star is crushed into a singularity. Some kind of *cosmic egg* or *ylem* (pronounced *I-lem*) may possibly have once existed. However, nowadays most cosmologists suspect that it didn't. They realize that the universe might originally have contained only a few grams of matter, or perhaps none at all.

According to Einstein's famous equation $E = mc^2$, matter and energy are equivalent. This allows us to add matter and energy together and to speak of the total matter-energy content of the universe. When we do this, we get a number that is relatively small, or perhaps even zero. There is an enormous quantity of matter in the universe. The same can be said for energy. But most of the energy is negative. As far as we can tell, the two quantities are approximately equal. Adding them together is like adding +1 and -1 to get zero.

Most of the energy in the universe is gravitational

energy. Gravity is much weaker than the other known forces, but it is the only one that acts over large distances. We can neglect all of the heat energy in the universe, as well as the electromagnetic energy, the energy in radioactive nuclei, and so on, because they make only tiny contributions to the total.

In order to see why gravitational energy is always negative, suppose that we wanted to move some massive body, such as an asteroid, out of the solar system. This would obviously require the expenditure of a great deal of energy. Thus we can conclude that a body has less energy when it is relatively close to the sun than it does when it is far away. But if it is moved so far away that it can no longer feel the sun's gravitational influence, its energy must be zero. Consequently its original energy must have been negative, a quantity *less* than zero.

Every gravitating body in the universe attracts every other, and gravity acts in a myriad of different ways. To cite just one example, our galaxy and those near it are currently being drawn toward a massive cluster of galaxies that is known as the *great attractor* at a velocity of hundreds of kilometers per second. Gravitational forces not only bind planets to stars, and cause the formation of groups of galaxies, they act upon the expansion of the entire universe. When the associated energies are added together, one winds up with a huge negative number. The quantity of matter is represented by a large number too, a positive one. As far as anyone can tell, they cancel one another out.

Of course, it is not possible to say that they are *exactly* the same. When one large number is subtracted from another, there may be a small but finite result. If I have a billion dollars, and lose approximately all of it in the stock market, I may be left with a few dollars. But it will be hard to tell whether my net worth is now slightly positive or slightly negative. Keeping track of every last penny is what made accounting so tiresome in the days before computers.

What all this means is that no one can prove that the universe is a "big nothing" in which positive matter and negative energy balance one another out exactly. But it very well might be. And this possibility has led to numerous kinds of speculation about the universe in recent times.

During the greater part of this section, I have concentrated on the things that can actually be observed, and on facts that can be deduced from these observations. The exceptions were my brief account of the inflationary universe theory and the discussion of the implications of a measurable cosmological constant. One hears so much of the inflationary theory these days that leaving it out of my discussions would have created a misleading picture of current thought in cosmology. And it would hardly be possible to give an accurate account of scientists' knowledge of the universe while leaving out what may turn out to be a significant recent discovery.

But at least the inflationary theory and ideas about an accelerating expansion depend to a certain extent on observation. In this chapter I propose to go a bit further and to briefly discuss some matters that are pure speculation. My excuse for doing this is that if I ignored these ideas it would be impossible to say anything about the origin of our universe. But when you read my accounts of them, you should remember that the scientists who conceive these ideas only talk about what *might* be true. In no case is there any empirical evidence to support their theories.

The best known theory about the origin of the universe is one that was developed by Stephen Hawking with physicist James Hartle of the University of California at Santa Barbara. According to this proposal (Hawking is careful not to call it a theory), which was described in Hawking's book, *A Brief History of Time,* the universe may not have had a beginning; it may have had its origin in *imaginary time*.

I suspect that many of the readers of Hawking's book

were misled by this term. He was using the term *imaginary* in a mathematical sense that bears little relation to the word as it is used in ordinary language. What Hawking meant was that, early in the history of the big bang, the dimension of time had the character of a spatial dimension. The universe did not have a beginning because, if one goes back far enough, time no longer exists. Instead, one has three spatial dimensions and one that is spacelike.

As Hartle has pointed out, if one makes this assumption, the theoretical universe that results looks very much like the one that we observe today. But this is no proof that imaginary time ever existed. The proposal is likely to remain nothing more than an interesting idea. Naturally this has not prevented Hawking from pursuing the idea further. He has suggested, for example, that matter that reaches the singularity in the center of a black hole may move through imaginary time, bud off, and form an entirely new universe. If these "baby universes," as Hawking calls them, really exist, it might never be possible to detect their existence. They would not exist in our space and our time, but in a set of dimensions of their own. Sometimes I suspect that no one but Hawking really believes this idea (and I am not sure that he does either). But there seems to be no way to prove that his hypothesis is wrong.

Most of the other speculation about the origin of the universe views time in a more conventional manner. It is often said that there was nothing *before* the big bang because time and space originated together. All that may be needed for the creation of a universe is the sudden appearance of a tiny bubble of expanding spacetime.[1] This bubble may contain little or no matter. But as the expansion continues, positive matter and negative energy will rush in to fill the ever-expanding space.

Scientists know of no reason why such bubbles of spacetime might not be created spontaneously. New universes may be popping into existence all the time like bubbles in a carbonated drink. But until a theory of quantum gravity—one that combines the general theory of relativity with quantum mechanics—is found, no one will know whether this can happen or not. As I write this, there exists no theory that is capable of describing what was going on at the moment of creation.

Some theories discuss the creations of such bubbles within a specific context. For example, in Andrei Linde's theory of chaotic inflation, which is an elaboration of the inflationary universe theory, tiny portions of our universe may suddenly begin to experience inflationary expansions. If they do, they will quickly grow into new universes in their own right. Again, if this really happens, we will most likely never be able to observe this phenomenon. The new universes are presumed to separate themselves from our universe in a tiny fraction of a second. According to Linde, universes may continually be budding off in this manner. And of course our universe may have had this kind of origin. It may be an offspring of some previous universe.

Naturally, if this idea is correct, the total number of distinct universes would be very large, possibly even infinite. Naturally not all of them would survive for very long. It is possible that some would collapse in big crunches when they had hardly gotten started. But even if this happened in an infinite number of case, there might be an infinity of universes left that bore a resemblance to ours. If this were the case, we would expect that some would contain life.

Linde's idea is only one of many variations on the many-universe hypothesis. Cosmologists and physicists have suggested a number of ways in which our universe might have come into being. It might have begun with the creation of just two subatomic particles, for example. According to the laws of quantum mechanics, particles can spring into existence out of nothing. They appear in complementary pairs, an electron and a positron, for example. Normally they disappear again within a tiny fraction of a second. However, this might have been just long enough to get a universe going. If they didn't vanish immediately, they would have to occupy a bubble of spacetime, which would then spontaneously grow.

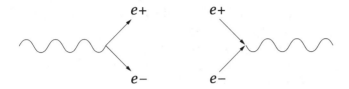

FIG. 10: *The creation and destruction of real and virtual particles. Einstein's famous equation $E = mc^2$ tells us that matter can be created from energy and energy from matter. In* FIG. 10A, *a gamma ray (energy) is converted into two particles, an electron and a positron. Since one is positively and the other negatively charged, the net charge is still zero. In* FIG. 10B, *an electron and a positron collide with one another and produce a gamma ray.* FIGS. 10A *and* 10B *show the creation and destruction of real particles. Virtual particles (*FIG. 9C*) can be created for brief periods of time when the required energy is not available. Here, electron-positron pairs are created and destroyed, but there are no gamma rays. Many different kinds of particles can be created and destroyed in this way. Electrons and positrons provide only one example.*

According to yet another hypothesis, our universe began when the familiar four dimensions (three of space and one of time) suddenly crystallized out of some multidimensional spacetime. There is nothing very bizarre about this idea. Or at least it is no stranger than the Hartle-Hawking notion that things got going when time separated itself from the three spatial dimensions and took on its familiar character.

It is even conceivable that an advanced technological civilization could create universes at will. Presumably, all that would be needed would be the ability to create tiny spacetime bubbles. In order to accomplish this, it might be necessary to focus very large amounts of energy into a very small volume. But an advanced technology might provide the means for doing this. According to an old physicists' joke, our universe might be some graduate student's experiment gone wrong.

One thing that makes the various many-universe hypotheses appealing is that they would explain why our universe is so hospitable to life. If there are numerous universes, the laws of physics in every one would not have to be the same, and there could be many universes in which life never had a chance to exist.

Alternatively, our universe might have been designed to support life. If it was, I just hope that God doesn't turn out to be that incompetent graduate student.

NOTES

[1] Spacetime is another word that causes needless confusion. In general relativity, the universe is viewed as having three dimensions of space and one of time, just as it is in Newtonian physics. The only difference is that, in relativity, space and time interact with one another in various complex ways. Scientists speak of spacetime simply because considering space or time by itself would involve leaving out an essential ingredient. Newton's laws describe the behavior of objects in spacetime too. But in his theory, space and time were independent.

THE SEARCH FOR A THEORY OF MATTER

"WAS IT A GOD THAT WROTE THESE SIGNS?"

By around 1800, scientists had studied numerous natural phenomena and forces of nature, including electricity, magnetism, gravity, light, and heat. But they had attained only a partial understanding of some of them. Gravity was understood. To be sure, some were bothered by the idea of attraction at a distance; they did not see how distant bodies could affect one another. However, even they had to admit that Newton's law accurately described the motions of the planets and other astronomical bodies, as well as the behavior of objects near or on the surface of the earth. Benjamin Franklin, the American printer, statesman, and scientist, had proved that electricity had one component, not two. That is, positively and negatively charged objects seemed to contain a greater or lesser amount of a single electrical fluid.[1] No one knew what caused objects to become magnetized, but the forces exerted by magnets could be measured, as could the forces between electrically charged objects. Finally, scientists were beginning to realize that light was not composed of particles, as Newton had thought; it was a wave phenomenon. No one could say what the waves were composed of. However, light seemed to possess properties analogous to those of sound or water waves.

It seemed only natural to wonder if there might be some connection between these various phenomena. After all, there was only one force—gravity—that acted upon celestial objects. To be sure, many of them, such as the sun and the stars emitted light, while others, like the moon, reflected it. But light had no effect on their motions. Why then should many forces be encountered in a terrestrial environment? Might they not somehow be related to one another?

The first step toward an understanding of the forces was

taken by the Danish physicist Hans Christian Oersted. In 1820, Oersted discovered that if an electrical current was set up in a wire, it would deflect a compass needle that was placed nearby. He did not stumble upon this result by accident. Convinced that electricity and magnetism were somehow related to one another, he had decided to test this idea by making the appropriate experiments. Thus he was able to show that an electrical current produced a magnetic field.

The next step was taken by the British physicist Michael Faraday, who is considered to be one of the greatest scientists of his century. Faraday is unique among physicists in that he understood little of mathematics. Born in 1791 as the son of a blacksmith, he had been apprenticed to a book binder at the age of thirteen. He quickly developed an interest in science and, at the age of twenty-one, he won a post as an assistant to Sir Humphrey Davy, a chemist who was one of the most famous scientists of the day. At first, he devoted himself to chemistry. By the time he was forty, he had established an international reputation in that subject. But, by 1830, he was beginning to spend more time on physics than on chemistry. Today, it would be virtually impossible to switch fields in this manner. There is simply too much that has to be learned to master each discipline. However, in Faraday's time, physics and chemistry were not considered to be distinct subjects. On the contrary, they were viewed as different parts of natural philosophy. And of course neither field had acquired the complexity that it has now.

While he was still working primarily in chemistry, Faraday became convinced that, if an electrical current could produce a magnetic field, the opposite should also be the case. There had to be some way that magnets could induce a current in a wire. He wrestled with the problem for ten years, and made numerous experiments, all of which ended in failure. Finally, in 1831, he thought of trying to induce a current, not in a straight length of wire, but in one that was wound into a coil. During a few months of work around the end of that year, he made significant progress, and succeeded in constructing the first dynamos, electrical generators, and transformers. According to an old story, which is probably apocryphal, William Gladstone, the great liberal who was later to be prime minister of England four times, asked Faraday what the uses of his discoveries were. Faraday is said to have replied, "At present I do not know, but one day you will be able to tax them."

Faraday's discoveries did not cease in 1831. Convinced that the various forces of nature had a common origin, he began to wonder if electricity or magnetism might not have some effect on light. At first, again, his experiments were unsuccessful. Then, in 1845, he succeeded in demonstrating that a magnetic field could influence the behavior of a beam of light.

By 1845, it was known that light was made up of what physicists call transverse waves. The direction of the vibrations of which light is composed can have various different orientations. For example, if a ray of light is coming to you from the north, it can vibrate in an east-west or in an up-down direction, or in any direction in between. There is nothing very esoteric about this phenomenon. Something similar is seen in ocean waves. As the waves move toward the shore, the individual water molecules move in an up-down direction. If this were not the case, there could be no wave crests or troughs. An ocean wave will move inland when it encounters a shoreline. But in the open sea, water only moves in an up-down direction. Water waves are only one example of a variety of wave phenomena that are found in nature. Sounds, for example, are produced by waves of compression in the air. When we listen to speech, or to music, or hear the dog barking, individual air molecules do not make their way from the speaker to our ears. Only the wave does this.

Ordinary light is made up of waves of all possible orientations. In the example given above, it will usually be a mixture of east-west, up-down, and other orientations. Normally the mixture remains unchanged. However, certain crystals have the ability to alter the character of light that passes through them. The light that they transmit emerges with vibrations in certain preferred directions. Such light is said to be polarized.

In 1845, Faraday found that a magnetic field could change the direction in which a light beam was polarized. For example, if the light waves originally had an up-down orientation, interaction with the magnetic field would cause them to acquire a polarization in a slightly different direction. Clearly, light and magnetism were related. And if light could be affected by magnets, it must have some relationship to electricity as well.

The discoveries that Faraday made were among the most important of his era. But, hampered by his ignorance of mathematics, he was able to go only so far. Today, it is not possible to be a physicist without knowing a great deal of mathematics. Even in Faraday's day it was difficult. Faraday had the success he did only because he had a vivid visual imagination that allowed him to create such concepts as magnetic *lines of force*.[2] Interestingly, these lines of force can be given a mathematical interpretation, and it turns out that Faraday's ideas were almost always correct. Knowing no mathematics, he made use of his vivid visual intuition instead.

But the next step could only be taken by a scientist with a great deal of formal mathematical training. That would be the Scottish physicist James Clerk Maxwell.

ELECTROMAGNETISM

Maxwell was the greatest theoretical physicist of his era, and his contributions ranged over almost the whole of physics. It was he, for example, who proved by theoretical calculations alone that the rings of Saturn had to be made up of tiny particles. It was only in our time that scientists were able to make observations that confirmed the correctness of his analysis, when the spacecraft Pioneer II crossed Saturn's rings.

Maxwell's scientific contributions were numerous. He published his first scientific paper at the age of fourteen, and his later work was of such importance that scientists generally rank him with Newton and Einstein. Maxwell elaborated upon ideas advanced by other scientists about the mechanisms of color vision in human beings, and made the world's first color photograph in 1861. He applied ideas about probability and statistics to the behavior of collections of moving molecules, and derived laws that explained the properties of gasses. He made important contributions to the branch of physics known as thermodynamics, which deals with the phenomena of energy and heat.

But Maxwell's greatest achievement was his electromagnetic theory, which was first published in a scientific paper in 1861, and later summed up in his *Treatise on Electricity and Magnetism* (1873). Maxwell began by putting Faraday's visual ideas about electricity and magnetism into mathematical form. When he did this, he was able to find four simple equations that summed up all that was known about these two phenomena. But Maxwell did more than summarize existing knowledge. He had a flash of insight that told him a changing electrical current should produce a magnetic field, a phenomenon that had never been observed. When Maxwell put this idea into mathematical form, he found that there should exist a kind of radiation that was composed of changing electric and magnetic fields. When Maxwell calculated the speed at which this radiation would travel, he found that it would have the velocity of light. Thus he concluded, correctly, that light was made up of oscillating electric and magnetic fields that vibrated in a direction perpendicular to the light's motion. The relationship between light and electromagnetism is so close that it is actually possible to measure the speed of light in experiments in which no light is propagated. One needs only make the appropriate electrical measurements. This is not a very difficult task, by the way. It is sometimes done as a university classroom demonstration.

Maxwell's equations have never become as familiar to the general public as Einstein's $E=mc^2$ and (to a lesser extent) Newton's $F=ma$ (force equals mass times acceleration) have. The equations are relatively simple, but they are differential equations that are expressed in the language of calculus. However, it is not difficult to summarize their content. The equations can be expressed in words as follows:

1. An electric charge produces an electric field.
2. The poles of two different magnets exert a force on one another.
3. Electric fields are produced by changing magnetic fields.
4. Magnetic fields are produced by electric currents *and* by changing electric fields (the second half of this equation was Maxwell's insight).

Naturally Maxwell's equations are quantitative in nature. Equation 1, for example, not only says that an electric field is produced, it also allows physicists to calculate the strength of the field, and the force between two charges. Like all useful equations in physics, one can put numbers into them, and get other numbers out.

Maxwell's equations eventually led to the formulation of Einstein's theory of relativity. It was not by chance that Einstein's first paper on relativity was entitled "On the Electrodynamics of Moving Bodies." Einstein found that if he made certain reasonable assumptions, then Maxwell's equations would take on a form that allowed one to come to a number of very surprising conclusions. Maxwell's equations can, in fact, be considered to be a part of Einstein's theory of relativity.

Maxwell's achievement did not receive anything resembling universal acclaim during his lifetime. When he died at the age of forty-seven, many physicists were unsure that his theory was correct. And there were others who simply failed to understand it. Praise was not entirely lacking, however. Quoting Goethe, the German physicist Ludwig Boltzmann, a contemporary of Maxwell, asked, "*War es ein Gott der diese Zeichen schrieb?*" (Was it a God that wrote these signs?)

In modern times, physicists have been unstinting in their praise of Maxwell's work on electromagnetism. Einstein may have summed it up best when he called Maxwell's theory "the most profound and the most fruitful that physics has experienced since the time of Newton." What he meant was that Maxwell not only explained the phenomenon of electromagnetism, he also transformed physics by demonstrating the importance of the idea of fields. Today scientists commonly speak of gravitational fields, and of fields associated with subatomic particles, as well as the fields of electromagnetism. Without this idea, much of modern physics would not exist. And of course this change of outlook can be attributed to the impact of Maxwell's work. Before his time, physicists spoke only of forces between individual objects.

HOW TO CHANGE THE WORLD

Maxwell's was not just a theoretical achievement. It also had significant practical results. If light was electromagnetic radiation, then it followed that other kinds of radiation, with different wavelengths, should exist. This idea was confirmed when the German physicist Heinrich Hertz discovered radio waves in 1866. Then, in 1896, after two years of experimentation, the Italian physicist Gugliemo Marconi showed that it was possible to communicate by means of radio signals. The world had already begun to change.

Today, Maxwell's legacy influences almost every aspect of our lives. It was his theoretical innovation that ultimately made modern electronics possible. And he accomplished this because, sometime around the middle of the nineteenth century, he began to wonder what the precise relationship between those two forces called electricity and magnetism was. Naturally, if there had been no Maxwell, someone would have discovered the equations of electromagnetism sooner or later. But Maxwell's insights into the nature of electricity and magnetism caused this to happen sooner. If he had never been born, modern electronic technology would not have blossomed as rapidly as it has.

NOTES

[1] Today we know that there are both positively and negatively charged particles. But this does not contradict Franklin's finding. When an object is electrically charged, it has an excess or deficit of negatively charged electrons.

[2] There is a common school experiment in which iron filings are placed on a sheet of paper under which a magnet is placed. If the paper is jiggled a little, the filings will align themselves along magnetic force lines.

CHAPTER 1

TOO MANY PARTICLES

By around the beginning of the twentieth century, physicists thought they had everything figured out. There were two forces in nature, gravity and electromagnetism. They explained everything, at least in principle. The electron had been discovered in 1897, and atoms were believed to be composed of negatively charged electrons and some kind of positively charged matter. Theories had been developed that explained the emission of light and other kinds of electromagnetic radiation by vibrating electrons. Electromagnetism also explained the properties of matter. Solid matter existed because molecules were held together by electromagnetic forces. No one knew precisely how these force operated, but that was one of the details that would eventually be worked out. The properties of gasses seemed even easier to explain. A gas was made up of rapidly moving molecules that constantly collided with one another and the walls of any container in which they might be enclosed. Heat was obviously a property of rapidly moving molecules. The hotter an object became, the more rapidly its constituent molecules moved. And of course light was nothing other than a kind of electromagnetic vibration. Physics, these scientists thought, was nearly a closed subject. No one pursued Faraday's idea that there might be some connection between all of the forces of nature. Physicists knew that electromagnetism and gravity were similar in some respects. For example, electric and magnetic forces could cause objects to be attracted to one another, just as gravity did. But they did not think that this was something that had to be explained. After all, there was no reason why there should not be two unrelated forces in nature.

Today, this point of view seems to have been naive and

shortsighted in the extreme. But it really wasn't so unreasonable. After all, gravity and electromagnetism are the only two forces that we encounter in our everyday lives. The presence of light allows us to see, and sound—waves of compression in the air—makes it possible for us to hear. The existence of sound was a consequence of the properties of gasses and the details of the interactions between the molecules in a gas seemed to have been more or less adequately worked out. Physicists could explain why objects such as tables and chairs seemed solid. To be sure they were mostly empty space. Molecules occupied only a small part of the volume of such objects. However, the electromagnetic forces between the molecules prevented solid objects from penetrating one another. The fact that one couldn't stick one's hand through a table was not very surprising.

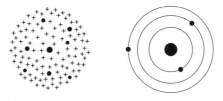

FIG. 1: *The old and new conceptions of the atom. Before the atomic nucleus was discovered in 1911, atoms were conceived of as spheres of positive charge in which negatively charged electrons were embedded. This was known as the "plum pudding model." The electrons were the plums and the positive sphere the pudding. When the discovery of nuclei made this view untenable, atoms came to be conceived of as made up of electrons that orbited the nucleus.*

Then, suddenly, everything began to change. In 1900, the German physicist Max Planck showed that matter did not emit light continuously, as Maxwell's electromagnetic theory said it should. On the contrary, light was emitted in the form of little packets of energy that Planck called *quanta*. In 1905 Einstein generalized Planck's idea by suggesting that light actually traveled through space in the form of particles (which we now call *photons*), which corresponded to Planck's quanta of energy. Naturally Einstein was aware that light had a wave character. What he was saying was that light could be could be made up of particles and waves at the same time. It sounded paradoxical. But Einstein was able to show that certain kinds of experiments led inevitably to this conclusion.

During the next two decades, one discovery followed another. In 1911, the British physicist Ernest Rutherford discovered the atomic nucleus, and in 1913 the Danish physicist Niels Bohr proposed his quantum theory of the atom. The work of Rutherford and of Bohr led eventually to the discovery of quantum mechanics in 1925. The new theory had a character that sometimes seemed very strange, but it did appear to explain the behavior of matter at the subatomic level.

Not one, but two seemingly different quantum theories were proposed at this time. The German physicist Werner Heisenberg formulated a very abstract, highly mathematical theory, which was called *matrix mechanics*, while the Austrian Erwin Schrödinger proposed a more intuitive formulation in which matter was viewed as being made up of waves. Neither Heisenberg nor Schrödinger liked the other's theory. Heisenberg called Schrödinger's theory "crap," and Schrödinger expressed the opinion that Heisenberg's method was "disgusting." However it was soon proved that the two theories were mathematically equivalent to one another. Although they looked very different, they always led to the same conclusions.

It was immediately recognized that there was something very paradoxical about quantum mechanics. For example, if the theory was correct, light and matter alike had to have both wave and particle characteristics. But one could not observe both at the same time. An electron, for example, would behave as a wave in one experiment and as a particle in another. But it was not possible to observe both properties simultaneously. It was as though the observer forced it to take one characteristic or the other. And, as though that was not bad enough, the theory seemed to imply that a particle could be in more than one place at the same time (a phenomenon that has actually been observed in modern experiments). Nevertheless, quantum mechanics was apparently a correct theory; it made numerical predictions that could be confirmed very accurately by experiments.

Some of the paradoxes of quantum mechanics remain unresolved today. Or at least it has become apparent that a number of different interpretations of the picture that it paints of subatomic reality are possible. No one understood what quantum mechanics really *meant* in 1925, and no one does today. However, it is perfectly possible to use quantum mechanics to make mathematical calculations without worrying about philosophical interpretations, and this is precisely what most physicists do. From the very first, quantum mechanics has proved to be an extremely successful theory. Today, it is the foundation of almost all of modern physics.

When quantum mechanics was discovered, the world of physics did not become significantly more complicated, however. In 1925, scientists still knew of only two fundamental forces. And they had discovered only two subatomic particles: the electron and the proton. The hydrogen atom consisted of an electron that orbited a proton. More complex atoms could be explained simply by assuming that more orbital electrons were present, and that both electrons and protons were present in the nucleus. This seemed to explain why, for example, a carbon nucleus weighed twelve times as much as a proton but only had six times the electrical charge. According to ideas that were accepted at the time, the carbon nucleus contained twelve protons and six electrons, and the positive charges of six of

the protons were canceled out. 12 – 6 =
as that.

No one knew what the force was that he،
cles together. The only thing that was obvi८
couldn't be electromagnetism. Electromag.
cause the positively charged protons to repel o.
not to stick together. Like charges cause repuls،
unlike (one positive and one negative) electrical
attract. There had to be something which overca،
protons' electrical repulsion.

So, even though it was sometimes hard to make sens
quantum mechanics, physicists' conception of matter w
not greatly altered. They still believed that there wer
two basic forces. It appeared that there might be some
unknown third force that acted only at the atomic level. But
there seemed to be little doubt that this problem would be
cleared up eventually. Matter was still thought to be made
up of protons and electrons. To be sure, it was now necessary
to admit the existence of photons too. But photons were
associated with light. They were not components of atoms.

THE NEUTRON

But then, in 1932, this simple conception of matter began to
change. In that year the English physicist James Chadwick
discovered the neutron. The neutron had not been seen
previously because it was electrically neutral and was
therefore unaffected by the electric and magnetic fields to
which particles were subjected in experiments. Fortunately, the discovery of this new particle didn't create any
new problems. On the contrary, it cleared one up. Calculations done with quantum mechanics had seemed to indicate that electrons would not remain confined within
atomic nuclei. They moved too rapidly to remain bound.
But if a nucleus was made up of protons and neutrons
there was no problem.

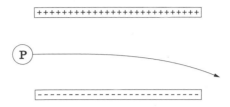

FIG. 2: *The deviation of a charged particle in an electric field. In the example shown here, a proton passes between two charged plates. It will veer toward the one that is negatively charged. A magnet field will also cause the path of a charged particle to become curved. Neither electric nor magnetic fields have any effect on the path of a neutron, which, as the name implies, is electrically neutral.*

Unfortunately—or at least it was unfortunate for those physicists who believed that they now possessed a nice tidy conception of the constituents of matter—a number of additional particles were discovered in the years that followed. In the same year that Chadwick discovered the neutron, the American physicist Carl Anderson discovered positrons—positively charged electrons—in cosmic rays. Unlike protons, neutrons, and electrons, positrons were not a component of ordinary matter. Physicists were beginning to realize that there was more to the subatomic world than they had thought.

And then, in 1936, various investigators of cosmic rays began to see a new, negatively charged particle that had a mass between that of the electron and that of the proton. Called the mesotron at first, it is now known as the muon, after the Greek letter *mu*. Muons have properties similar to that of the electron, but are 207 times heavier. But the similarity between the muon and the electron was not apparent at first. In fact, there was a great deal of confusion about the nature of the new particle. But, in order to see why this confusion existed, it will be necessary to backtrack a little.

THE PUZZLE OF ACTION AT A DISTANCE

When Newton proposed his law of universal gravitation in 1687, many of his contemporaries were troubled by the problem of action at a distance. They did not see how two distant bodies could influence one another. They were familiar only with forces between objects that came into contact. Newton's gravity, they said, was the kind of "occult" quality that scientists had been laboring to get rid of. Here, *occult* was not used in the modern sense, but rather in the sense of *hidden* or *invisible*. The scientists of the day were beginning to demand that physical concepts should refer to things that could be seen or measured. Though they knew that gravitating bodies attracted one another, they did not see how gravitational force could propagate through empty space. Hence it was regarded as something *occult*.

Newton had no ready answer. He could reply only that he "made no hypotheses." What he meant was that he could calculate what the gravitational attraction between two bodies was, but did not know how gravity acted. He was as much in the dark as his critics.

The problem was not really cleared up until a development in quantum mechanics known as quantum field theory came along. As this elaboration of quantum mechanics was worked out, beginning in the 1930s, physicists began to realize that attractive and repulsive forces could be explained by the action of particles. It is the photon that transmits electromagnetic forces. For example, two negatively charged electrons will repel one another. According to quantum mechanics the repulsive force comes about because each electron will emit photons that are absorbed by the other. An analogous situation would be one in which two ice skaters throw a heavy ball back and forth. As each one throws or catches the ball, they move a little farther away. The thrower feels a certain amount of recoil, and the skater who catches the ball is pushed backwards.

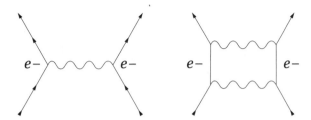

FIG. 3: *Repulsive forces between charged particles. Two electrons repel one another when they exchange electrons. Two simple examples are shown here. In* FIG. 3A, *the electrons exchange one photon, and in* FIG. 3B *they exchange two. These diagrams are called Feynman diagrams after the American physicist Richard Feynman, who invented them.*

The exchange of photons also explains attractive forces between particles with unlike charges, such as the electron and the proton. Here the situation is not appreciably more complicated, but the analogy breaks down. To be sure, it is possible to invent a more contrived analogy in which the skaters stand back to back and throw a boomerang to one another. This would presumably cause them to move toward, not away from, each other. But this idea is probably not terribly illuminating.

The photons that charged particles exchange are never observed. Nevertheless, they are very real. Theories that explain forces in terms of particle exchange have experimental consequences, and they have been tested to a high degree of accuracy in the laboratory. There are things in physics that cannot be observed directly. Yet experimental proof of their existence can be quite convincing. The phenomenon of photon exchange is just one of many possible examples.

Gravity is also explained by the exchange of particles, hypothetical ones called gravitons. Unlike photons, which can at least be seen when they are emitted in the form of light, gravitons have never been observed. It is not yet possible to devise experiments capable of detecting them. However, few physicists doubt their existence.

And what does this have to do with the muon? Well, in 1935, the year before the muon was discovered, the Japanese physicist Hideki Yukawa proposed a theory according to which the nuclear force was caused by the exchange of particles called mesons. According to Yukawa's theory, the meson would have a mass about 200 times greater than that of the electron. The muon, or mesotron as it was called then, seemed to fit the bill perfectly.

It was discovered only later that the muon did not have the right properties to function as a carrier of the nuclear force. The true meson was discovered by the English physicist Cecil Powell in 1947. It was named the pi meson to distinguish it from the particle discovered earlier. The name has since been shortened to *pion*.

The discovery of the pion raised the question of why the muon should exist. It wasn't a constituent of ordinary matter. If all the muons in the universe were suddenly to disappear, most of us would never know the difference. Muons are seen only in experiments carried out by physicists. Describing it as a "heavy electron" didn't help. Although it was possible to form hydrogenlike atoms made of protons and muons, these didn't exist in nature. All that physicists knew was that the world of subatomic particles was somewhat more complicated than they had initially thought.

THE FOUR FORCES

Scientists now knew, not of two, but of four forces in nature. There was gravity, electromagnetism, a *strong* force that bound nuclear particles together, and also a *weak* nuclear force. In order to understand how the conception of the weak force came about, it will be necessary to delve a little more into history.

Within a few years after radioactivity was discovered by the French physicist Henri Bequerel in 1896, it had been established that radioactive atoms emitted three different kinds of radiation. These were called alpha, beta, and gamma after the first three letters of the Greek alphabet (if, by now you've gotten the impression that physicists use Greek letters a lot, you're absolutely correct). It was soon established that alpha rays were actually heavy particles made up of two protons and two neutrons. They were identical with the nuclei of helium atoms. Beta rays turned out to be nothing other than electrons, and it was established that gamma rays were a form of high-energy electromagnetic radiation. At the time, physicists did not understand how or why these various kinds of radiation should be emitted. And, in the case of beta rays, there was an additional problem.

The alpha and gamma radiation emitted from a particular atom always had the same energy. For example, alpha particles given off by uranium-238 always have the same velocity and hence the same energy of motion. But this is not the case with beta emission. Some of the electrons that are thrown off by a given variety of radioactive atom have more energy than others. Furthermore, the variation is continuous. The electrons emitted by a radioactive element can have *any* energy within a certain range. One electron may be 5 percent more energetic than another, while a third may possess 40 percent more energy. The energy may be anything from a quantity that is almost zero up to some maximum.

It was not easy to understand why this should be the case. A radioactive decay, it was thought, should always produce the same amount of energy. But in the case of a slow-moving electron, some of the energy had somehow disappeared. A possible solution to the problem was proposed by the Austrian physicist Wolfgang Pauli in 1930. Pauli suggested that part of the energy created in the radioactive decay was carried off by the electron, and part by a hitherto-unseen particle that he called the neutrino. Pauli's neutrino had zero mass,[1] and it traveled at the speed of light. Naturally there was no difficulty in understanding how different neutrinos could have different energies. The photon, after all, also lacks mass. Yet a photon of ultraviolet light is more energetic than one of visible light, and an X ray photon has more energy yet.

After Pauli suggested the existence of the neutrino, he suffered a few pangs of conscience. "I have done the worst thing for a theoretical physicist," he said to his colleague, the German astronomer Walter Baade. "I have invented something that can never be detected experimentally." Pauli's neutrino, if it really existed, would have to be a particle that almost never interacted with matter. A neutrino should be capable of passing through the entire earth without hindrance.

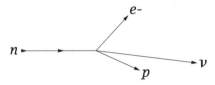

FIG. 4: *Beta decay. Here a neutron decays into three particles: a proton, an electron, and a neutrino. The neutrino is represented by the Greek letter nu.*

Yet the neutrino finally was detected in an experiment performed by the American physicists Clyde Cowan, Jr. and Frederick Reines in 1956. Cowan and Reines set up an experiment next to a nuclear reactor at Savannah River, South Carolina. They reasoned that, if neutrinos really existed, then the reactor should give off 10^{18} (a billion billion) of them every second. Most would experience no interactions, but if a few did, there was a good chance that they could be seen.

Neutrinos are the most common particles in the universe. Billions of them pass through our bodies every second. Yet, like the muon, they are not constituents of ordinary matter. Neutrinos do not exist within atomic nuclei; on the contrary, they are created in the process of beta decay. In certain radioactive nuclei, one of the neutrons will sometimes be transformed into an electron, a proton, and a neutrino. The electron can be observed as a beta ray, and the transformation of a neutron into a proton changes the nucleus into the nucleus of a different chemical element.

Many physicists were skeptical of Pauli's theory when it was first proposed. The Italian physicist Enrico Fermi, on the other hand, approached the problem in a more open-minded manner. If the neutrino really existed, he reasoned, then it should be possible to develop a theory that would describe beta emission. When Fermi did this, he found that it was necessary to assume the existence of a fourth force of nature, one that was different from the gravitational, electromagnetic, and strong forces. Fermi's force is now called the weak nuclear force, or simply the *weak force* for short.

If Fermi's and Yukawa's theories were correct, then there were, not two, but four basic forces in nature. Experiments performed over the following decades showed that this conclusion was correct. Fermi introduced the weak force in 1933, and as I write this during the late 1990s, physicists still believe that there are four fundamental forces. Of these, gravity is the weakest. It is important because it has a range that is essentially infinite. Distant galaxies exert a gravitational pull on one another, and gravity affects the expansion of the entire universe. The electromagnetic force also has an infinite range. But this fact has little practical significance. All bodies, including stars, planets, and galaxies, are electrically neutral. If one did somehow acquire a charge, it would quickly lose it. A positively charged object, for example, attracts electrons that then cancel out the excess charge. Planets like the earth, and galaxies as well, possess magnetic fields. But these fields are very weak compared to those that can be produced in the laboratory. The earth's magnetism, for that matter, is not very strong compared to that of a magnet that a child might play with. If the magnet is brought near a compass needle, the needle points to the magnet, not to the earth's magnetic poles.

The strong force is about 10^{39} (this number can be represented by the numeral 1 followed by thirty-nine zeros) times as strong as gravity, but its range is very limited. At distances greater than the diameter of an atomic nucleus, its intensity rapidly falls off to zero. The weak force has a greater range, roughly equivalent to the diameter of an atom (about one hundred times larger than a nuclear diameter). But it too quickly fades away to nothing at distances greater than this. The weak force, incidentally, has a strength that is about one-hundred thousandth of that of the strong force. Hence its name.

Between the years 1930 and 1935, the world of subatomic physics became somewhat more complicated than it had been in 1900, or even in 1915. Not only were there now four known forces rather than two, the number of particles had increased from two to seven: the proton, the neutron, the electron, the neutrino, the positron, the photon, and the *mesotron* (as we have seen, at this point, scientists had not realized that the muon was not the meson predicted by Yukawa).

As it turned out, this was to be only the beginning.

TOO MANY PARTICLES

During the 1930s, physicists began to experiment with particle accelerators, devices that could make use of magnetic or electric fields to accelerate charged particles to velocities approaching that of light. The first such device, the cyclotron, which was built by the American physicist Ernest Lawrence in 1930, made use of magnetic forces. The first cyclotron was quite small; it had a diameter of only a few inches. But it was soon succeeded by larger models constructed by Lawrence and other physicists. By the end of the decade, thirty-five cyclotrons were in use and numerous others were under construction.

There were limits to the velocities to which particles could be accelerated in a cyclotron. But, during the 1940s, the basic design was refined and modified in a variety of different ways. Thus a new generation of larger, even more powerful machines was inaugurated. Today, accelerators are often very large. For example, the one at the Fermi National Accelerator Laboratory (often called *Fermilab*) in Batavia, Illinois, has a diameter that is more than a mile. And, as I write this, a larger and even more powerful accelerator is being constructed at CERN (Centre Européen pour la Recherche Nucléaire) in Switzerland. CERN is an international endeavor supported by a number of European nations.

When particles that have been accelerated to high energies are made to collide with one another, enormous quantities of energy are released. When I say *enormous* I mean, of course, that they are large compared to energies normally seen on the subatomic level. The energies created by particle accelerators, however, reside in individual particles. A nuclear reactor is a large device. A particle accelerator may also be physically large, but it probes the structure of matter at dimensions far smaller than that of an atomic nucleus (which is about one ten-trillionth of a centimeter). As a result, many different kinds of nuclear reactions take place, and numerous new particles are produced. For example, if two protons collide, they may be transformed into a charged pion and a deuteron (a composite particle composed of one electron and one neutron). Free pions don't remain around for long. They quickly decay into other particles. For example, the neutral pion (pions can have a positive or negative charge, or none at all) decays into two gamma rays. However, they exist for long enough a time that their presence can be detected.

As the amount of available energy is increased, the reactions become quite complex. During the 1940s, physicists discovered numerous new particles, including, as we have seen, the true Yukawa meson. By the end of the 1950s, hundreds were known. The new particles typically had very short lifetimes; many of them existed for less than a trillionth of a second. In the jargon of particle physics, they were often referred to as *resonances* rather than as *particles*. However, it was not possible to deny that they were real, however short-lived they might be.

PROBLEMS, PROBLEMS

It soon became apparent all was not well. Physicists had begun by trying to explain the properties of atoms and atomic nuclei in terms of a few particles. But the number of known particles had multiplied beyond all reason. It might have been possible to conclude that there were seven basic particles in the universe. But hundreds? They obviously couldn't all be elementary. To make matters worse, some of them behaved in unexpected ways, refusing to decay into other particles as quickly as they should have. Physicists even invented a property called *strangeness*. Although strangeness could be described mathematically, and although physicists began to understand why some particles were strange, this didn't bring much order into the field of particle physics.

To make matters worse, no one knew what the nuclear force was. Meson theory was really no great help. When Yukawa had formulated his theory, he had to make a guess about the nature of the force that held neutrons and protons together. His guess was good enough to give some results that could be confirmed experimentally. Mesons did indeed exist, and they had masses approximately equal to those predicted by his theory. Nevertheless, there were circumstances in which Yukawa's theory failed utterly; when tested by experiment, some of its predictions proved to be hopelessly wrong.

Physicists did know that the nuclear force was unlike gravitational and electromagnetic forces. The gravitational force between two bodies and the forces between two electric charges or magnetic poles are all described by inverse square laws. These forces fell off as the square of the distance between two objects. For example, if one has two electrical charges or two gravitating bodies, the force between them diminishes by a factor of four if they are moved twice as far away ($2 \times 2 = 4$, and 4 is thus said to be the square of 2). Similarly, if the bodies are moved three times as far away, the force is one-ninth as great (because $3 \times 3 = 9$, and an *inverse* square law gives a factor of one-ninth).

But the law of nuclear force, whatever it was, could not have this form. If two protons, two neutrons, or a neutron and a proton were moved away from one another, the force between them did not diminish in this manner. There was a point at which it dropped rapidly to zero. This is why we say that the strong force (which I have been calling the *nuclear* force) has a range of about 10^{-13} centimeters.

During the 1960s, some progress was made in this area. Various approximations of the nuclear force were introduced. But it was obvious that they were just that, approximations. Physicists still did not know the mathematical form of the true force, or why it had the properties that it did.

The physicists of the 1950s and 1960s found themselves in a position that was not unlike that of astronomers in the days before Copernicus introduced his heliocentric system, in which the planets moved, not around the earth, but the sun. The world of subnuclear particles was very complicated, more complicated than it had any right to be. And no one knew exactly why things worked the way they did. To be sure, some physicists suggested that most of the new particles were only different energy states of some that had previously been known. But this really didn't help much. Physics is a mathematical science, and introducing a new verbal description of a complicated situation does little to further understanding. If matters were to be cleared up, a bold new approach was needed. But it was anything but obvious what this approach should be.

NOTES

[1] The neutrino was generally assumed to be massless until 1998, when experiments showed that it probably had a small mass after all, one that was much less than that of the lightest particle known up until that time, the electron.

EINSTEIN'S
UNIFIED FIELD THEORY

Shortly after Albert Einstein published his general theory of relativity in 1915, he began to think abut the possibility of a unified field theory, one which would combine gravity and electromagnetism. At the time, there was every reason to think that such a theory might be possible. After all, gravity and electromagnetism were still the only known forces. Furthermore, they were similar; in both theories, attraction and repulsion were long range forces. Like electric and magnetic forces, gravity could be described by an inverse square law if it was not too intense.[1] Einstein realized that gravity and electromagnetism might only be different aspects of a single physical reality.

Einstein worked on his unified field theory for the rest of his life. When he died in 1955, he still had not achieved success. To be sure, there were times that he thought he had found the answer. In 1925, for example, he published a theory, only to repudiate it later. He began to have doubts almost as soon as it was published. In a letter written to the Austrian-Dutch physicist Paul Ehrenfest, he said, "I have once again a theory of gravitation-electricity; very beautiful but dubious." Later the same year, he described the theory as "no good."

Einstein continued to publish papers on the unification of the gravitational and electromagnetic fields throughout his life. But he never found what he was looking for. And by focusing on this subject, he isolated himself from other physicists who were exploring the new worlds of quantum mechanics and of elementary particles. Many of his contemporaries believed that he was wasting his life. Indeed, they may have had a point. Einstein's last important contributions to physics were made in the years 1924 and 1925.

After that he became obsessed with a quest for what most of his contemporaries thought was a chimera.

Although Einstein never found what he was seeking, it is worthwhile to describe his attempts in some detail. Today, the problem of unification has become central to physics, and some of the paths that Einstein followed anticipated an outlook that became common half a century later. What I have in mind is Einstein's use of an extra dimension of space. He wondered if a unified theory of two forces could not be formulated in five dimensions (four of space and one of time). Today, physicists are attempting to combine all four forces in ten- and eleven-dimensional theories.

Einstein actually approached the problem in two different ways. He began by trying to formulate a theory in the usual number of dimensions that generalized his theory of gravity. This was a monumental task. Compared to the Newtonian theory of gravity, general relativity is mathematically very complicated. In Newton's theory, the strength of a gravitational field depends upon just one quantity, the size of a gravitating mass. If the mass of a body is doubled, the gravitational force that it exerts on other bodies will also be increased by a factor of two. In general relativity, on the other hand, the gravitational field has ten different components, and they can interact with one another in a complex manner. General relativity is mathematically so complicated that no general solutions to Einstein's equations have ever been found. The equations can only be solved in special cases where certain simplifying assumptions are made. Fortunately, many of these describe situations that are of great physical interest. For example, it is not so difficult to calculate the gravitational fields in the vicinity of the sun. Here, one has a nearly spherical mass, and the gravitational forces are great enough that, for all practical purposes, the effects of the various planets can be neglected.

If this were not bad enough, Einstein faced another problem. There were no experimental findings to guide him in his quest. Maxwell was able to formulate his theory of electromagnetism because numerous experiments involving electric and magnetic forces had been made. Newton was led to his theory of gravity by noting that there were certain similarities between the motions of celestial bodies and the motion of bodies near the surface of the earth. Once he realized that the same force—gravity—was at work in both cases, he was able to work out mathematical equations that described it.

Einstein had a more difficult problem. No experiments had ever been performed that showed a connection between gravity and electromagnetism. Thus he had no choice but to try one mathematical scheme after another in the hope that he would eventually discover one that worked. And of course he failed.

Thus he shifted his attention to five-dimensional theories. When he failed to achieve success, he went back to his original approach. He was to waver back and forth between one technique and the other for the rest of his life. When he failed to achieve success with one, he would go back and take another look at the other. And then he would shift back to the first again.

THE "FOURTH DIMENSION"

At one time, science fiction writers frequently made use of the concept of a *fourth dimension*. The premise of their stories was that four dimensions of space actually existed, but that we were aware only of three. This particular story-telling technique isn't much used any more. In fact, it is now regarded as something of a cliche. But it does raise the question of whether such an unseen dimension could possibly be real.

As it turns out, it is possible to state unequivocally that

there isn't. For example, it can be proved mathematically that if the number of spatial dimensions were greater than, or less than, three, then stable planetary orbits would not be possible. The earth and the other planets would either fly off into space, or they would spiral into the sun. The fact that this has not happened can be taken as proof of the fact that we live in a three-dimensional world.

To be sure, physicists often speak of four-dimensional *spacetime* when they discuss Einstein's relativity theories. But this is not the same thing. In relativity, there are still only three spatial dimensions. The fourth dimension is time. The reason that physicists speak of spacetime is that, in relativity, space and time interact with one another. Hence it is difficult to look at one without taking consideration of the other. However, it should be born in mind that Newtonian physics is just as four-dimensional as Einstein's. The only difference is that it is easier to separate space and time and to speak of them individually.

Naturally Einstein knew that our world had three spatial dimensions. Yet he attempted to create theories in which there were four. At first glance, he seems to have been involved in a contradiction. In order to explain why he was not, it will be necessary to go back to the year 1914, when the Finnish physicist Gunnar Nordström proposed a five-dimensional theory in which he attempted to unify the forces of gravity and electromagnetism. Nordström's theory soon had to be discarded because it was inconsistent with experimental facts. For example, it did not explain the bending of light rays that grazed the surface of the sun, a phenomenon that was observed in 1919. On the other hand, Einstein's four-dimensional theory of general relativity did explain this. In fact the 1919 experiment was performed in order to test Einstein's prediction that this effect should be large enough to be seen.

Then, in 1919, the Polish physicist Theodor Kaluza formulated another theory, one which was a generalization of

Einstein's theory. In those days, a scientific paper could not be published unless it was endorsed by a well-known physicist. Consequently, Kaluza, who was only a *privatdocent* (a kind of assistant professor), sent his paper to Einstein. Einstein was impressed by some of Kaluza's ideas, but he suggested to the latter that more work should be done before the paper was published. He felt that Kaluza's arguments in favor of the theory were not convincing enough, and that attempts should be made to show how it could be confirmed by experiment.

Nothing happened for two years. Then, in 1921, Einstein became aware of an attempt by the German mathematician Hermann Weyl to unify gravity and electromagnetism in a somewhat different manner. Finding Weyl's theory even more unconvincing than Kaluza's, he recommended the latter for publication.

As soon as it was published, it was apparent that there were a number of defects in Kaluza's theory. The theory was unable to explain quantum phenomena (this is a point I will return to shortly), and it was not clear whether the extra dimension was to be understood as something that was physically real, or only as a mathematical fiction. It was not at all apparent how these defects could be remedied.

Then, in 1926, the Swedish physicist Oskar Klein suggested a possible explanation for the fact that Kaluza's fifth dimension was not observed. According to Klein, it might be "compacted," rolled up into dimensions much smaller than that of an atomic nucleus. Compacting a dimension would be something like rolling a sheet of paper up into a cylinder and then twisting it tighter and tighter. As one does so, the circumference of the cylinder becomes smaller and smaller. If the process could be continued indefinitely, one dimension of the two-dimensional sheet of paper would become so small that it would be invisible. The cylinder would become something that looked like a one-dimensional line.

There is no reason why all of the dimensions of our universe must have the same character. If one of them is compacted, then the circumference of the universe in one direction would be infinitesimally small. In such a case, we would not know that this dimension was there; it would be too tiny to see. Except on the submicroscopic level, the familiar three dimensions of space and one of time would be the only ones that had any significance. Thus in Kaluza's five-dimensional universe, the planets could have stable orbits. And the extra dimension would not throw monkey wrenches into any other area of macroscopic physics.

Einstein was interested enough in this idea that he did some further work on Kaluza's theory. But there apparently was no way that he could make the theory work. He abandoned his efforts and went back to looking for a generalization of general relativity. Yet, the idea of a five-dimensional universe was one to which he was to return again and again.

THE QUANTUM WORLD

Einstein was always skeptical about quantum mechanics. He did not deny that it was an enormously successful theory that produced predictions that could be confirmed by experiment to a high degree of accuracy. Nor was he especially bothered by the wave-particle duality. After all, he had been the first to suggest that light might have particle as well as wave characteristics. What Einstein objected to was the idea of indeterminism that was inherent in the theory.

For example, quantum mechanics can explain the phenomenon of radioactive decay. It adequately describes the emission of an alpha or beta particle, or a gamma ray. But it does not tell us when such a decay will happen. According to the theory, this is purely a matter of chance. All that we can say is that there is, for example, a 50 percent chance that a radioactive nucleus will emit an alpha particle in some period of time. Similarly, one can use quantum mechanics to predict the wavelengths of light that will be emitted by an atom. But nothing can be said about when this will happen. The emission of radiation is seen as a spontaneous event.

Throughout his life, Einstein attempted to show that there was something inherently contradictory about quantum mechanics. His arguments with the Danish physicist Niels Bohr are especially well known. Time after time, Einstein would invent a line of reasoning that seemed to show that the theory of quantum mechanics could not be correct. Time after time, Bohr would find an answer. Today, it is generally thought that Bohr won the argument. However, Einstein's conviction was not swayed. To his death, he insisted that "God does not play dice with the universe."

One of Einstein's motivations for seeking a unified field theory was the hope that such a theory would explain the apparent indeterminism of quantum mechanics. A unified field theory, he thought, might explain quantum phenomena and restore causality to the subatomic world. Today we can say that his quest was simultaneously somewhat quixotic and an anticipation of theoretical work that has been done at the frontiers of physics at the end of the twentieth century. As we shall see in the last chapter of this part, physicists are again attempting to unify the forces of nature, and they are trying to do so with theories that postulate extra dimensions of space. They hope to find a theory that will finally explain the nature of quantum phenomena. Unlike Einstein, they don't think that determinism will thereby be restored. But they do hope to discover why certain subatomic particles exist, and why they possess the properties they have.

Einstein died in 1955 of an aneurysm of the abdominal aorta. Though he had been ill for some time, he had never stopped working on the quest for a unified field theory.

After his death, some manuscript pages were found by his bedside containing work that he had done on the theory just before he died.

NOTES

[1] In general relativity, Newton's inverse square law no longer holds in general. However, Newton's law of gravitation turns out to be a good approximation in most cases.

CHAPTER 2
THE HUNTING OF THE QUARK

I've never met California Institute of Technology's Murray Gell-Mann. I did see him once, however, at a memorial for the late physicist Richard Feynman. Gell-Mann, who was the first to speak, began by remarking that he had never quite been able to approve of Feynman's lifestyle before he went on to discuss the latter's achievements in physics.

Feynman and Gell-Mann had offices near one another at Cal Tech. Feynman's flamboyance didn't sit well with Gell-Mann, who is known for his conservative dress and lifestyle. However, Gell-Mann's contributions to physics have been anything but conservative. It was his innovative thought in the field of theoretical particle physics that finally brought order to the chaotic "particle zoo" that had been puzzling physicists for so long.

In order to understand precisely what his contributions were, it will again be necessary to backtrack a bit. Suppose that you were confronted with a large collection of mysterious objects. Suppose that some were reasonably familiar, and that you had no idea what many of the others were for. How would you proceed if you wanted to find some order in the unruly mess you were contemplating? Well, chances are that you would begin by looking for similarities between certain of the objects so that you could group them together. You might not learn very much by doing this, but at least it would be a start.

This is exactly what physicists did with the numerous particles that they had discovered. And when the particles were grouped together according to their observed properties, patterns began to emerge. No one knew why these patterns existed, but recognizing them led to some progress. It even became possible to predict the existence of as-yet-undiscovered particles. For example, Gell-Mann and physicist Abraham Pais of the Institute for Advanced Study in Princeton, New Jersey, did just this when they suggested in 1954 that two new particles must exist if the classification schemes then in use were to make any sense. These particles were detected experimentally in 1956 and 1959.

Another step forward was taken in 1961 when Gell-Mann and Israeli physicist Yuval Ne'eman independently discovered a scheme that would allow certain kinds of heavy particles, including the proton and the neutron, to be grouped into subfamilies. Gell-Mann called this grouping the *eightfold way* because an important group—which included the proton and the neutron—had eight members. He wasn't implying that there was any connection between particle physics and eastern philosophy (the original eightfold way was the Buddha's prescription for attaining enlightenment). Like many physicists, he enjoyed inventing colorful names for important theoretical ideas.

The next step, naturally, was to try to understand why this particular classification scheme should work. If the known particles fit naturally into groups of eight, and groups of ten, and so on, there had to be some underlying reason why they did. Gell-Mann and, independently, the American physicist George Zweig, soon suggested a possible answer. The scheme would work if these particles were composed of even smaller subparticles, which Gell-Mann called *quarks*. Zweig called them *aces*, but it was Gell-Mann's name that stuck. His contributions to physics had been more numerous than Zweig's, and physicists followed his lead. The fact that Gell-Mann's name was more colorful may also have been a factor. The name *quark* had been taken from James Joyce's *Finnegan's Wake*. Most likely, most of the physicists who used the name had never read Joyce's book. However, there was more of a poetic ring to *quark* than there was to *ace*.

At first, many physicists doubted that quarks really existed. For one thing, they had fractional charges, which had never been observed in nature. The proton and the electron have electrical charges which are taken to be +1 and −1 respectively. Physicists had seen atoms that had gained two electrons and thus had a charge of −2, and they had seen charges of +2 as well. But no one had ever observed a particle that had a charge of $1/4$ or $1/2$ or $1/3$. Nevertheless, if Gell-Mann and Zweig's theory was to work, quarks had to have a charge of $1/3$ or $2/3$ (or $-1/3$ or $-2/3$ when they were negative charged). According to the theory, the proton was composed of two positively charged quarks with charges of $+2/3$ and a third quark with a $-1/3$ charge. Simple addition and subtraction ($2/3 + 2/3 - 1/3$) gave a sum of +1. The neutron, on the other hand, which is electrically neutral, was supposed to be made up of three quarks whose charges added up to zero. The quark theory also appeared to explain the properties of mesons, which presumably had two quark components rather than three. It appeared that, strange as the idea was, it was something that had to be taken seriously.

But were quarks real? Initially, many physicists regarded them as nothing more than a useful mathematical fiction. Their suspicion seemed to be confirmed when experimental searches for quarks failed. Experimental physicists looked for quarks in cosmic rays, in rocks, and even in seawater. But these experiments always produced negative results, even though they went on for more than twenty years.

However, an experiment performed at the Stanford Linear Accelerator Laboratory (SLAC) in 1968 gave more positive results. When electrons were accelerated to high energies in a two-mile-long tube and made to collide with protons, it was revealed that the proton appeared to contain three pointlike charges. This was precisely what the quark theory predicted.

However, a problem remained. If quarks were real, why were they never observed to exist in a free state? Electrons, protons, and neutrons, which are ordinarily components of atoms, can be detected individually. For example, if an electron absorbs enough energy, the force that binds it to the atomic nucleus will be overcome, and it will go flying off on its own. Why should the quark behave any differently?

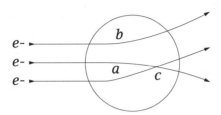

FIG. 5: *Detecting quarks. If electrons are accelerated to high enough energies they can penetrate protons and neutrons and "look inside." In the SLAC experiment, the deviations of the paths of the electrons allowed physicists to conclude that protons and neutrons each contained three pointlike particles. This was the first experimental proof of the existence of quarks.*

The theorists got to work, and theories were developed that indicated that beyond a certain point the forces between quarks would increase, not decrease, with distance. The quarks were permanently bound within neutrons and other particles. And if a very great quantity of energy were supplied, this still would not break them apart. New quarks would be created instead, and these new quarks would bind themselves together just as tightly as the original ones did. The creation of quarks in this manner is a consequence of Einstein's famous equation $E = mc^2$. The equation tells us that energy (E) and mass (m) are equivalent (c^2, the speed of light squared, is just a conversion factor). Since all matter, including quarks, has mass, it is possible to create particles out of energy.

Yet another step forward had been taken. Although physicists were still far from attaining a complete understanding of subnuclear matter. The discovery that quarks couldn't be pried apart said nothing about what the force between quarks was, or what mechanisms it depended upon. It was known only that it behaved differently than gravitational and electromagnetic forces, which always decreased with distance. And it didn't clear up the problem of the strong nuclear force, or the theoretical difficulties related to the behavior of mesons. It was clear that the strong force must be a secondary manifestation of the force between quarks. However, in practice, the physicists who did calculations concerning the nuclear force still had to use the only partially accurate approximations that they had relied upon before.

QED

Sometimes finding the solution to a problem requires knowledge of the past. Physics did possess a successful quantum theory of the electromagnetic force, and of the interactions between light (i.e., photons) and particles of matter. Called *quantum electrodynamics*, or QED for short, it had been investigated and refined over a period of decades. The theory had initially seemed to be seriously flawed. The physicists who worked with QED found they could obtain results that were roughly correct if they carried out their calculations only to the first approximation. But if they attempted to obtain more accurate results, matters suddenly became worse, not better. If calculations were carried out to higher approximations the equations "blew up" and infinite quantities appeared. The theory predicted, for example, that the mass of the electron should be infinite, which was obviously not the case.

In 1948 Richard Feynman, the American physicist Julian Schwinger, and the Japanese physicist Shin'ichiro Tomonaga independently discovered a method called *renormalization* (remember that word; I'll be referring to it again later) for getting rid of the infinities in QED. It was not at all obvious that the method was mathematically consistent,[1] but it worked! In fact, it worked very well. QED has yielded predictions that have been verified by experiment to an accuracy of better than one part in 10 billion. It is Feynman's method, incidentally, that is most often used today. Though the other two turned out to be mathematically equivalent, his scheme was more intuitive and easier to use.

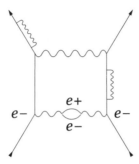

FIG. 6: *A Feynman diagram. There are an infinite number of different possible Feynman diagrams, and some of them become quite complicated. This one is another example of a possible repulsive reaction between two electrons. Note that photons that are emitted by an electron can be absorbed by the same electron; they do not always have to be exchanged. As a photon travels from one electron to the other, it may spend part of its journey as an electron-positron pair. Even more complex cases are possible.*

After QED was made renormalizable, the following situation existed: Physics had a theory of gravity, Einstein's general theory of relativity. There had long existed a workable theory of the electromagnetic force. But the strong and weak forces were still only partially understood. The weak force could be described by Fermi's theory, but this theory was only approximately correct. It gave correct results under certain circumstances, and failed in others. The nature of the strong nuclear force (the term *strong force* can be used either to describe the force between nucleons or the more fundamental force between quarks) was still unknown. Obviously, there was still a lot of theoretical and experimental work to be done.

In 1967, the American physicist Steven Weinberg and the Pakistani physicist Abdus Salam independently proposed a theory of the weak and electromagnetic forces. This theory not only solved the problem of the weak force, but it also was the first step toward the unification of all four of the forces. The *electroweak theory*, as it was called, initially suffered from the same kind of problem that had plagued QED, that of the appearance of infinite quantities. However, in 1971 the Dutch physicist Gerhard 't Hooft showed that the theory could be renormalized.

And then, in 1983, three new particles that the theory predicted, designated by the letters W and Z (there were three because the W could have either a positive or negative charge, while the Z was always neutral) were discovered experimentally. Naturally physicists rejoiced.[2] The first step toward fulfilling Einstein's dream, the unification of the forces, had been achieved.

Finally, during the 1970s theoretical physicists worked out a theory called *quantum chromodynamics*, or QCD, which described the force between quarks. Where the electromagnetic force depended upon two different kinds of electrical charge, called positive and negative, the behavior of quarks was such that three were required. The three quark *charges* were given the names *red*, *green*, and *blue* in analogy with the three primary colors of light.[3] Naturally these names should not be taken literally. Quarks are far smaller than the wavelengths of visible light. Hence they have no color. Here, *red*, *green*, and *blue* are just names. The three quark charges could just as well have been called Fred, Wilhelm, and Andrea, or even Rupert's Dry Cleaning, Antonio's Pizza, and Café D'amour. Using color names is more convenient, however. When the three primary colors of light are mixed, white light is produced. When the three quark charges are added, the total charge disappears. The proton, for example, which contains three differently colored quarks, is said to be *colorless*. This is analogous to the case of an atom, where positive and negative charges cancel out to produce an object that is electrically neutral.

The force between quarks is caused by the exchange of particles called gluons. They play a role analogous to that of the photon and the W and Z particles. Like quarks, gluons have color. The strong force (that name is used to describe the forces between quarks as well as those between nuclear particles) is therefore somewhat more complicated than the electroweak force. However, even though calculations are sometimes arduous, they can be performed and the results can be tested by experiment. QCD has become a well-verified theory.

Today, it is known that there are actually six different kinds of quarks, called *up, down, strange, charmed, bottom,* and *top.* Only the up and down quarks, which are found in protons and neutrons, are constituents of ordinary matter. However, all six quarks have been detected in the laboratory. Naturally they are never seen in isolation. However, there are methods for determining when a particle has, say, a charmed or a bottom quark as a constituent.

Each of the six quarks comes in three different colors, so there are eighteen possible combinations in all. Quarks are the constituents of all of the heavy, proton or neutronlike particles that are seen in nature. There are also two electronlike particles call the muon and tauon. Both have masses much larger than that of the electron. Again, only the electron is part of ordinary matter. However its relatives have been observed in numerous experiments. There are also three different kinds of neutrinos. The muon neutrino (which is observed in reactions involving the muon) is distinct from the more familiar electron neutrino (the one that figures in beta decay) and from the tauon neutrino as well. Collectively, these six particles are known as leptons.

It appears, therefore, that there are twelve fundamental particles of matter: six quarks and six leptons. Particles such as the positron are generally not counted separately. The positron has properties that are similar to that of the electron. For example, its mass is exactly the same. The main difference is that the positron carries a positive charge. Differently colored quarks are not counted separately either. A red up quark behaves exactly as its green counterpart does. The only difference is in the charges that they carry.

The photon, the gluons, and the W and Z particles are not components of matter. They are particles of force. The photon differs from the others in that it can manifest itself as light. Thus there is one case where we can actually see one of the forces of nature. The force particles behave somewhat differently than those of matter. For example, they can be "squeezed" together in a way that matter particles can not be. It is this that makes it possible to create light beams of varying intensity. A very intense beam contains a greater number of photons than a weak one, though it occupies the same volume of space. This cannot be done with matter particles. One can't superimpose one table on another to get one that is twice as heavy, and it is not possible to create a super-dense nucleus by packing the protons and neutrons more tightly together.

Together, QED, QCD, the electroweak theory, and the catalogs of known particles constitute what is known as the standard model of particle physics. The validity of the standard model has been confirmed by thousands of experiments that have been performed all over the world. There have been a small number of experiments that suggest that it might not be 100 percent accurate. But the interpretation of these experiments is a matter of controversy. Thus, it is possible to say that, so far, the standard model has withstood the test of time.

Nevertheless, as I write this, physicists are attempting to

THE SEARCH FOR A THEORY OF MATTER

go beyond the standard model. They do not believe that it provides the final answers. Specifically, they believe that, if the electromagnetic and weak forces can be unified, then it should be possible to go even further, and to find a theory that explains all four of the forces of nature. They hope that, if this unification is achieved, it will bring with it a new understanding of the nature of force and matter, and that it will lead to new discoveries, just as Maxwell's unification of electricity and magnetism did over a century ago.

GUTS AND SUPERGRAVITY

After the electroweak unification had been developed, the obvious next step was to seek a theory that explained the electromagnetic, strong, and weak forces simultaneously. Initially, gravity was left out. The reason for this was that, although gravity appears to be very simple in the Newtonian inverse-square approximation, it becomes something very complicated in Einstein's general theory of relativity. It possesses properties that are not observed in the other forces. For example, gravitational force is created, not only by the presence of massive bodies, but also by the gravitational field itself. One could say that, in Einstein's theory, gravity itself gravitates. The existence of pressure also contributes to the gravitational force. As a result of these complications, gravity cannot be renormalized. General relativity is simply not consistent with such theories as QED and QCD.

Thus physicists began to seek a theory of just three of the forces. They reasoned that, if they were successful, then perhaps someone might think of a way that gravity could finally be included. But, as it turned out, they were a bit too successful. A number of different theories were created, but no one knew which, if any, of them was likely to be correct.

These theories were called *grand unified theories*, or GUTS. It is possible to parody Voltaire's quip about the Holy

Roman Empire[4] by saying that they were neither grand nor unified (no accounting was made of the force of gravity), and that none of them ever became established theories.

The GUTS probably tell us something about the nature of force and matter. There have been many theories that have turned out to be approximately correct under certain circumstances and terribly wrong under others. Fermi's theory of the weak force and the Yukawa meson theory are just two examples. Though the GUTS make certain predictions that have not been explained experimentally, they have shed light on certain matters, such as the relative absence of antimatter[5] in the universe.

When it was realized that the GUTS had achieved only limited success, physicists went back to one of the paths that had been pursued by Einstein. They began to take another look at theories in which the number of spacetime dimensions was greater than four. They didn't do this immediately. By this time, the original five-dimensional Kaluza-Klein theory had been forgotten, and Einstein had been so isolated from other physicists in his later years that few had paid much attention to his work on a theory involving an extra dimension of space. However, some of them eventually began to realize that this was exactly the kind of approach that might be needed

The first multidimensional theory, developed by a number of physicists during the 1970s, was called *supergravity*. Supergravity was based on an idea called *supersymmetry* (which physicists affectionately nicknamed SUSY), which was a new, more all-embracing way of grouping subnuclear particles together. This concept seemed to be very promising at first. It turned out that, if supersymmetry was indeed a property of nature, then gravity could be renormalized after all. But attempts to find a workable supergravity theory ultimately failed. Supergravity theory predicted the existence of particles that had never been seen. But this really wasn't a serious problem. In contemporary times, particles are virtually always predicted by theory before they are detected in experiments. Experimental techniques have become so complex that experimental physicists must know what to look for before they even begin to design an experiment. The difficulty was that supergravity did not seem capable of accounting for the existence of all the particles that were already known to exist.

It seemed that, at best, supergravity was another of those partially successful theories that seem to crop up so often these days. Many physicists still suspect that some of the predicted new particles will eventually be discovered. After all, even though supergravity failed to work, supersymmetry might be a real property of nature. However, it is necessary to accept the conclusion that, as a method of unifying the forces, supergravity failed.

NOTES

[1] When asked for what it was that he had received the Nobel prize, Feynman would often answer, "For sweeping some infinities under the rug."

[2] The confirmation of the theory created a problem of protocol. According to long-established custom, the wife of a Nobel prize winner is escorted into the ceremony on the right arm of the king of Sweden. When Salam won the prize, he naturally showed up with his two wives. I have been unable to discover what solution was devised. If the king had entered with one wife on his right arm and one on his left, this would have implied that the one on the left was somehow inferior. Possibly they were brought in by precedence of age.

[3] These are not the same as the three primary colors that are used in mixing pigments, red, yellow, and cyan (a kind of blue). The two processes work somewhat differently.

[4] He said that it was neither holy nor Roman, nor an empire.

5 I have not gone into the topic of antimatter in the preceding chapters. Hence a note of explanation is probably in order here. Every known particle has what is known as an antiparticle. For example, the positron is the antiparticle of the electron. Thus it is possible to conceive of a kind of matter in which positrons would orbit nuclei containing negatively charged antiprotons and neutral antineutrons (yes, there is an antineutron, even though it has the same zero charge as the neutron itself). The presence of antimatter is not observed in our universe, and the GUTs provide a plausible explanation of why this should be the case.

CHAPTER 3
SUPERSTRINGS AND OTHER ENTANGLEMENTS

In QED, the electron is viewed as a particle that has the dimensions of a mathematical point. Physicists realize that there is something very unrealistic about this, but they know of no solutions to the problem. The cures are worse than the disease. An electron cannot be pictured as a perfectly rigid sphere, because such a sphere would transmit signals at velocities greater than the speed of light, a violation of Einstein's theory of relativity. If a rigid sphere were "kicked" on one side, the impulse transmitted by the kick would travel right through it in zero time. Thus it would have infinite velocity. On the other hand, if an electron of finite size were not perfectly rigid, it could be deformed or broken apart. This would produce phenomena that are simply not observed. In the everyday world, even such hard objects as golf and billiard balls behave the way they do because they experience small deformations when hit.

Viewing the electron as something that is infinitely small causes QED to yield quantities that are infinitely large. For example, one cannot avoid the conclusion that both the mass and the charge of an electron are infinite. Since this is obviously not the case, something had to be done to avoid this conclusion. That *something*, renormalization, proved to be extraordinarily successful. However, renormalization makes use of techniques that are mathematically suspect. In physics, quantities are generally neglected because they are too small to make any difference, not because they are infinite and you don't want them.

So far, the standard model, which is made up of QED, QCD, and the electroweak theory, has worked very well. But the standard model cannot be a final theory. Not only does it make use of renormalization, it also fails to explain why particles have the charges and masses that they do. It does not tell us why there are six quarks and six leptons, or why the various forces have the strength that they do. For example, the strong force has a characteristic strength that is about 100 times greater than that of the electromagnetic force. Why should this factor be 100? Why not 4, or 25, or 1 million?

A THEORETICAL BACKWATER

Initially, physicists hoped that supergravity theory would provide some of the answers to these questions. But supergravity never fulfilled its promise. Therefore they began to look around for some other solution. As they did, they began to realize that some physicists who had been working in what seemed to be a theoretical backwater since the late 1960s might actually be onto something.

These physicists had been investigating theories that described particles—both particles of matter and particles of force—as tiny vibrating loops in multidimensional space time. At first, this work did not attract much notice. These theories required as many as twenty-six dimensions, and they did not explain why the extra dimensions were not observed. Furthermore, they seemed to contain inconsistencies. Interest in these *string* theories flared up for a while, and then subsided again.

But then, in 1974, the French physicist Joel Scherk and physicist John H. Schwarz of the California Institute of Technology showed that the multidimensionality of string theory was a virtue, not a defect. He showed, further, that if strings were pictured as tiny objects about 10^{-33} centimeters[1] in diameter, then the theory could be used to unify gravity with the other three forces.

This finding did not arouse much interest, however. At the time, the theories that made up the standard model seemed perfectly adequate. Theorists thought it more fruitful to pursue the idea that heavy particles were made up of quarks than to delve into what then seemed to be esoteric ideas. Thus, by the end of the decade of the 1970s, string theory was virtually forgotten.

But then, in 1984, everything suddenly changed. Schwarz and Michael Green of Queen Mary College in London showed that if string theory was combined with supersymmetry—the new method of grouping elementary particles together—then it was possible to eliminate certain mathematical inconsistencies that had plagued string theory from the beginning. Thus superstring (short for *supersymmetric string*) theory was born. Within a few years, superstring theory had become a major focus of theoretical activity around the world.

Superstring theory avoided previous difficulties by conceiving of particles, not as mathematical points, but as tiny vibrating loops. It was the superstring, not the individual particles that were fundamental. Particles were nothing but different modes of vibration of a string. They were analogous to the different notes that can be produced by a violin string when it is made to vibrate in different ways. The theory could also be used to explain particle interactions. Instead of viewing interactions between dimensionless objects, it created a picture in which individual loops could combine with one another to create a *bigger* loop. Loops could also split up into smaller ones, for example when a neutron decayed into a proton, an electron, and a neutrino.

But not all physicists were enthusiastic. Superstring theory showed promise but it yielded little in the way of results. It soon became apparent that although there were thousands of different possible formulations of the theory, only five basic superstring theories were possible. However the extra dimensions added a great deal of complexity. It became apparent that these dimensions could be intertwined with one another in numerous different ways.

There were other problems too. Although the concept of

superstrings was appealing, no one knew how to use the theory to predict the existence of the known particles. As I write this, the best that can be done is to use the theory to describe quarks and leptons in a very qualitative manner. And this is not enough. A successful theory of physics must be quantitative. It must be possible to put numbers in and to get meaningful numbers back out. For example, Newton's law of gravitation would not be of much use if it could not be used to calculate the orbits of the various planets.

And then there was the matter of the superstring's size. The smaller an object is, the greater the amount of energy required to observe it. Remember that it took an accelerator two miles long to give electrons enough energy to allow physicists to *see* inside protons and confirm the existence of quarks. In the case of superstrings, the situation was much worse. Simple calculations showed that even a particle accelerator the size of our galaxy might not generate enough energy to observe them.

Within the physics communities, opinion about the validity of the superstring concept was divided. Physicist Edward Witten of the Institute for Advanced Study has described superstring theory as "twenty-first century physics that was discovered by accident in the twentieth century." Others have called it "the only game in town." On the other hand, Richard Feynman bluntly branded superstring theory as "nonsense," and Nobel laureate Sheldon Glashow compared it to "medieval theology." His point was that, although superstring theory might be mathematically beautiful, no one knew how to compare it to experiment.

Glashow's point, although expressed derisively, is an important one. At the beginning of the twentieth century, physicists performed experiments, and then tried to find theories that would explain the results. During the middle decades of the century, theory began to predict the existence of particles that were discovered only later. By the end of the century, theory had outrun experiment to such an extent that theoretical physicists found themselves dealing with entities that could not possibly be seen in any experiment. In fact, as I write this, superstring theory and its spin-off, *membrane theory* (to be discussed shortly), have not produced a single prediction that can be put to experimental test. This was why Glashow spoke of "medieval theology." In his view, a large number of theoretical physicists had distanced themselves from the real physical world.

Naturally superstring theorists disagree. In their opinion, superstring theory represents the only chance we have of discovering how the universe really works. They have no desire to go back to the standard model, which accurately predicts experimental results, but which they view as something "very ugly." The point they are making is that the standard model is a patched-together affair that cannot possibly enlighten us about the fundamental nature of reality.

THE END OF PHYSICS?

On the other hand, superstring theory convinced many equally eminent physicists that their science might be nearing its end. Or at least some of them expressed this idea during the euphoria that accompanied the discovery of the theory. The idea is that, if a successful theory that unified all four of the forces of nature were found, it would be a *theory of everything*. All of physics could, in principle, be reduced to that theory. Physicists would know why the observed particles existed, and why they had certain observed properties. They would know why the various forces behave the way that they do. They would understand the nature of spacetime itself, and gain insight into the origin of our universe.

I don't mean that physicists would cease to exist. There would still be a lot of work to be done. Exploring all the implications of such a theory might take decades. Even after that task was accomplished, there would be plenty of work for new Ph.D.s. Finding a theory of everything would be like learning the rules of chess. Someone who accomplishes that has a long way to go before he becomes a grandmaster.

If such a theory could be found, all this could happen. However, a big question is contained in the small word *if*. Theories in physics have always been approximations. For example, Newton's law of gravitation describes gravity in an approximate way. As long as gravity is not too intense, it is a perfectly adequate theory. For example, an astronomer would be crazy if he tried to use anything but Newton's law to calculate the orbit of a comet. The small corrections that would be introduced if he used general relativity instead would be far too small to be measured. However, under certain circumstances, Newton's law breaks down, and general relativity has to be used. General relativity, too, has its limits. For example, it cannot describe the nature of spacetime at the level of the superstring, 10^{-33} centimeters. Nor can it tell us what was happening at the time of the creation of the universe.

So it is possible that a truly unified theory, whether it is a superstring theory or something else, will turn out to be an approximation too. It is possible that a theory of everything may never be found. For all we know, physical reality may be like the layers of an onion. If physicists manage to penetrate the first few, they may find that there are countless numbers more.

Can the universe be summed up in an equation or a set of equations? John Archibald Wheeler, an eminent physicist who was a student of Bohr's and Feynman's professor, doesn't think so. "I can't agree that there's any magic *equation!* [his emphasis]" he says. And of course, at this point, no one can prove that he is wrong. Surprisingly, some of the physicists who work with superstrings agree. Unlike their colleagues, they say that we have no way of knowing whether or not the concept of superstrings will lead to a final, all-embracing theory.

So far, I have been describing superstring theory in a rather general way, and have avoided discussing some of the "hot topics" (but I will go into some of these in the latter part of this chapter) that have become the center of discussion while I am writing this. After all, the work that is done at the frontiers of physics is constantly changing, and I didn't want to write a book that would be out of date as soon as it was published. However, I will probably be on safe ground if I mention a number of reasons why the quest for a unified theory might go on for a long time.

The mathematical complexity of superstring theory and the fact that numerous different theories are possible are two reasons. Even the most optimistic physicists admit that it might take decades to find a fully adequate theory and to explore all of its ramifications.

Another reason has to do with the nature of superstring theory, as it was practiced near the end of the twentieth century. As I pointed out previously, theory has far outrun experiment, and it might be a long time before scientists even know whether the concept of superstrings really describes what is going on in nature.

Recently, some scientists have pointed out that it might turn out that there are ways to test superstring theory after all. For example, if the compacted extra dimensions of space turn out to be larger than physicists have generally assumed, this fact could have observable results. It is possible that particles might sometimes fall into an extra dimension and "rattle" around. However, as I write this, no one is really sure how such an idea could be tested.

If superstring theory ultimately turns out to be incorrect, it does not necessarily follow that decades of theoretical labor will have been wasted. Theories that turn out to be wrong sometimes represent steps forward. When scientists know what doesn't work, they often have a better idea of what might be tried next. And, as we have seen, a great deal can sometimes be learned from theories that are only partially adequate. Yukawa's meson theory, Fermi's theory of the weak force, and the grand unified theories are just three examples.

FORCES AND PARTICLES

In modern physics, it is the forces (which physicists generally call *interactions*) that are most fundamental. Particles—both force and matter particles—are considered to be manifestations of fields of force that spread throughout space. But the physicists who work with superstring theory don't know what the basic fields are. They must work with the superstrings themselves, which are particles. Consequently they are a long way from being able to predict what the mass and charge of an electron should be, to cite just one example. I can't help but think of the tale of the blind men and the elephant. In this case, the superstring theorists have managed to grasp only the tail.[2] They are just beginning to discover what the rest of the animal might be like.

However, some tantalizing hints have been uncovered. For example, the dimensionality of spacetime may not be so fundamental a thing as scientists have always believed. As I write this, superstring theorists are investigating the properties of objects that might exist in spacetime of more than ten dimensions. Some of them seem to be as fundamental as superstrings themselves. Some physicists have even discovered a twelve-dimensional theory in which there are two time dimensions. It is not at all clear what it would mean to say that there was more than one dimension of time, but that is what comes out of the mathematics. This is not the only strange result. It has also been discovered that, in superstring theory, very small distances can be equivalent to very large ones. The structure of a tiny object in ten- or eleven-dimensional spacetime can mirror that of the entire universe. Not all of the findings have been this odd and surprising, however. For example, it has been found that the five basic superstring theories may only represent different aspects of a single, more fundamental, theory. Also, links have been found between superstring theory and supergravity. This may explain why supergravity gave some results that were partially correct.

Theoretical physicists are beginning to find that, the more they learn, the more they realize how many things they don't know. They have become aware that they are venturing into a new world, the nature of which they have only begun to understand.

MEMBRANES

In 1962, the English physicist P. A. M.[3] Dirac, one of the founders of QED, created a theory in which the electron was viewed, not as an infinitesimal point, but as little bubble of small but finite size. Vibrations of the bubble, Dirac suggested, might explain electronlike particles, such as the muon. Dirac's theory really didn't work, but a similar idea is being explored today. Physicists are now exploring the properties of objects of two or more dimensions that are embedded in multidimension spacetime. These objects are called *branes*.

A superstring is one-dimensional. It may twist and turn in a multidimensional space, but it is conceived of as something that has the same number of dimensions as a straight line. Recall that, in the Euclidian geometry that is taught in high school, a line is conceived of as something without width, in analogy with a point, which has no dimensions at all. If a string has one dimension, all surfaces are two-dimensional. Both a mathematical sheet and a hollow sphere have this character, as did Dirac's bubbles.

The scientists who work with superstring theory have discovered that similar two-dimensional objects might exist in a spacetime of eleven dimensions. Since they do not necessarily close in upon themselves in the manner that a sphere or Dirac's bubbles do, they are called membranes. The existence of branes of more than two dimensions is also possible. I won't discuss them in detail, however, since their characteristics are similar to those of membranes. It might be mentioned, however, that one theoretical object that is of special interest is the five-brane, which has two more dimensions than a three-dimensional solid.

There seems to be a deep connection between branes and superstrings. The nature of this connection can be easily understood if one imagines a membrane wrapped around a rolled-up sheet of paper, becoming a cylinder. If the paper is rolled up more tightly, the diameter of the cylinder shrinks until it finally becomes a one-dimensional line. This is exactly the same analogy that I used when explaining the nature of the extra dimension in the Kaluza-Klein theory.

Naturally, membranes are less well understood than superstrings, and it would probably be a mistake to say too much about their properties. After all, in a theory like this, a conclusion that seems to be correct today could easily be overturned tomorrow. However, it does seem clear that membrane theory is capable of explaining why there are five basic string theories. If the extra, eleventh, dimension curls up in one way, one of the theories emerges. If it is shrunk in a different manner, one of the other ten-dimensional string theories is the result. Furthermore, the use of membranes may lead to some new ideas that will make it possible to perform meaningful experiments. As we have seen, the lack of any experimental support has always been a problem.

The physicists who work with membrane theory have only caught a glimpse of what its implications might be.

However, it seems accurate to say that a whole new world has suddenly been opened up, and the physicists of the early twenty-first century will find themselves trying to find ways to understand what membrane theory really is.

Some physicists say that superstring theory has *unraveled*, and that something new is taking its place. This may be something of an exaggeration. The study of strings has not lost its importance. It has simply been discovered that superstring theory may be part of something much larger. Whatever that *something* is, our ideas about the universe and the nature of physical reality could very well change dramatically in the years ahead.

NOTES

[1] Remember that 10^{-33} is the number 1 divided by 1033. Thus strings are 10^{20} (100 billion billion) times smaller than an atomic nucleus, which has a diameter of about 10^{-13} centimeters.

[2] After I wrote this, I discovered that Einstein had once made a similar comment about the physics of his day. The only difference was that Einstein spoke of the tail of a lion. I don't claim to have been thinking like Einstein, however. Allusions to the story of the blind men and the elephant have been made in numerous different contexts.

[3] The initials stand for Paul Adrien Maurice. But Dirac always used only the initials, and not even his closest colleagues knew his real name.

EPILOGUE

Around the middle of the nineteenth century, physicists began to try to understand the nature of those two mysterious forces, electricity and magnetism, and to try and see if there was any connection between them. When they did this, they started on a quest that has yielded one astonishing new discovery after another. As they probed the nature of matter, they began to understand the workings of the atom, and then the atomic nucleus. There were times when everything seemed to have dissolved into confusion. For example, when numerous new particles were being discovered during the 1950s, the American physicist J. Robert Oppenheimer went so far as to suggest that the Nobel prize ought to be given to someone who *hadn't* found any new particles in the preceding year.

But the confusion always dissolved, allowing physicists to take another step forward. The difficulties associated with understanding the behavior of atoms led to the discovery of quantum mechanics. And the problems associated with the existence of an unreasonably large number of different subnuclear particles led to the discovery of quarks. Puzzles concerning the nature of the various forces led to the creation of the theories that now make up the standard model: QED, QCD, and the electroweak theory.

Today, we may be witnessing the beginning of yet another revolution in physics. It is true that none of the ideas of the superstring or membrane theories have been confirmed experimentally. And it is possible that those theories might eventually have to be discarded and replaced by something even more seemingly bizarre. But the one thing that we can be sure of is that surprising new discoveries will be made. Even when a theory turns out to be terribly wrong, it often points the way to the correct path.

At the moment, superstring and membrane theories really do seem to be the "only game in town." No one has discovered any other reasonable way of going beyond the standard model. But this does not guarantee their ultimate correctness. As new and more powerful particle accelerators are built (the next generation will begin with one at CERN that is under construction as I write this, and which is due to become operational by 2005), experimental physicists will have the chance to peer more deeply into the nature of subnuclear reality too. And of course we cannot be sure what they will find. The theorists think that certain kinds of new particles will be seen. If they are not, current theoretical ideas may have to be revised.

But of course that is the story of physics. If nature did not have its mysteries, science would not exist.

/

THE SCIENTIFIC IMAGINATION

FOREWORD

The reader might wonder why this part, entitled *The Scientific Imagination*, should deal primarily with physics and with physicists. The reasons are simple. Physics is the most developed of the natural sciences, and it is the field that I know the best. It would have been possible to include commentaries on the workings of the scientific imagination in such fields as chemistry and biology. But little would have been gained. The creative mind works in certain characteristic ways whatever the field that is being studied. The subject matter may be different, but the workings of the human mind remain pretty much the same.

Not all of the theories or experimental discoveries described in this book turned out to be correct. The scientific imagination is not infallible; it sometimes goes astray. And there are theories that are not even wrong; they are not very scientific to begin with. Understanding the sometimes ludicrous errors that the human imagination can produce gives one a better understanding, I think, of the thought processes that led to discoveries that significantly increased our understanding of the natural world. This is, after all, the part of the book dedicated to the creative imagination, of its gropings, successes, pitfalls, and errors.

I will deal not only with the scientific imagination, but also with the evolution of physics during the twentieth century. It would be impossible to discuss one of these topics while ignoring the other. When this evolution is examined in detail, we find, not only that numerous discoveries have been made, but also that the ways of thinking about the universe have changed. In 1900, physics dealt only with phenomena that could be observed in the laboratory. New discoveries often depended upon visual observations. Even the atomic nucleus was discovered in this manner. In

1911, the British physicist Ernest Rutherford set up an experiment in which atoms of gold and other heavy metals were bombarded with alpha particles (charged particles made up of two neutrons and two protons). His assistants were then given the task of observing the flashes of light that were seen when the alpha particles struck fluorescent screens after "bouncing off" the atoms.

During the first quarter of the century, the science of physics advanced with unprecedented rapidity, and one new theoretical concept after another was introduced. But observation still kept up with theory. It was still possible to perform experiments in which the new theoretical concepts were tested, even though it became necessary to use apparatus that was much more complex than it had been in Rutherford's day. But by the end of the twentieth century, theory developed a tendency to leave experiment far behind. Physicists created one new theoretical world after another, and there was often no way of telling exactly what the relation between these new worlds and the reality in which we live really was.

Of course this is only a sidelight. My main purpose is to show how the scientific imagination operates, and the greater part of this part is made up of investigations of this topic. I have tried to show, for example, that style plays an important role in scientific discovery and that stylistic differences between scientists can be as great as stylistic differences between those who create our art and literature. I have also tried to demonstrate that, at times, scientists' creative insights become more important than empirical knowledge; a theory can sometimes be so compelling that it becomes generally accepted long before it has much experimental support.

Scientists rarely pay much attention to the history of their disciplines. Great discoveries become things that are summed up in textbooks, and little attention is paid to the struggles that led to each new advance. Perhaps this is as it should be. Science, after all, consists of fields in which creative men and women seek to discover something new rather than dwell on the past. However, anyone who is more interested in the workings of the creative mind is likely to view matters somewhat differently. He is more likely to be interested in knowing how these various discoveries came about. And of course an understanding of the theoretical struggles that have taken place in physics in the twentieth century allows us to better comprehend the nature of the theoretical work that goes on today, and to understand how physicists can take their newly created mental universes so seriously.

CHAPTER 1
INTUITIONS
OF A DEEPER REALITY

During the late sixteenth century, Galileo became a a firm believer in Copernicus' idea that the sun, and not the earth, was the center of the solar system. Galileo insisted that the earth moved, that it revolved around the sun while rotating on its axis. But how did he know that it did? It wasn't until 1851 that an experiment was performed that demonstrated that the earth did indeed rotate. In that year, the French physicist Jean Bernard Léon Foucault suspended a 62-pound pendulum from the dome of the Panthéon in Paris, and found that the rotation of the earth caused the motion of the pendulum to slowly deviate from its orignal path. As the earth rotated under the pendulum, the plane of its swing shifted.

Today we consider Galileo to have been a great scientist, and count his advocacy of the Copernican system among his acheivements. But, though Galileo made many arguments about the motion of the earth in his book, he could do nothing more than make the idea seem plausible. In his day there was no way to prove the proposition. In fact, some of the material in Galileo's book is simply wrong. For example, he believed that the tides were caused by the sloshing back and forth of the oceans in their basins as the earth moved through space. Galileo ignored the correct idea of his contemporary, the German astronomer Johannes Kepler, that the tides could be related to the motion of the moon.

It was Foucault who actually proved that the earth moved. Yet today his name is known to few people other than physicists. Perhaps there is some justice in this, since what he demonstrated was something that scientists and other educated people already knew. But, in the absence of experimental proof, how did they know? And how did Galileo know?

The very fact that I can ask such questions suggests that there is something wrong with our ideas of scientific method. Supposedly, scientists begin by making observations and collecting facts. Then they form hypotheses to explain these facts. Finally, they test their hypotheses by making experiments. The Austrian-British philosopher Karl Popper has refined this idea somewhat. In his first book, *The Logic of Scientific Discovery*, published in 1934, he pointed out that no theory could ever be conclusively proved to be true. No matter how many experimental tests it survived, there would always remain the possibility that future experiments could show flaws in a theory. According to Popper, theories could only be falsified. If a theory survived enough attempts to prove it wrong, it could be viewed as having been corroborated. According to Popper, physics was a science because attempts could be made to falsify its theories. Astrology, Marxist history, and Freudian psychology were not sciences because their theories were not falsifiable.

Popper's work has had an enormous influence on the philosophy of science. Nevertheless, it does not give a very accurate description of the ways in which scientists actually work. For example, experimental scientists generally do not set out to falsify a theory. In most cases, the motivation for performing experiments is the belief that the theory in question is probably true. And Popper said nothing about the ways in which scientific hypotheses were formed. But he did come up with a criterion that allowed scientists and philosophers to answer the question, "What, exactly, is scientific truth?"

I'll have little more to say about Popper. His theory is an example of good philosophy, but it casts little light on how scientific discoveries are made. And it does nothing to explain how it is that scientists can be so sure that their theories are correct long before attempts at falsification can be made. Galileo is not the only one who expressed this kind of faith. Albert Einstein became convinced of the correctness of his theories long before any experimental tests were possible. In fact, he sometimes expressed the opinion that if an experiment appeared to contradict the results that he had worked out mathematically, then it was the experiment that was at fault.

I naturally don't mean to imply that great scientists are always right, or that experiment is unimportant. Both Einstein and Galileo made scientific blunders. And we believe their theories, not because they were convinced of their truth, but because experiment has shown that they were indeed right. We believe that the earth moves around the sun because the evidence is incontrovertible. Similarly, we believe in the correctness of Einstein's theories because numerous highly accurate experiments have been performed that confirm them. My point is, rather, that there is more to scientific creativity than meets the eye. It does not depend simply upon the gathering of facts followed by the invention of hypotheses to explain them. In fact, the creativity of great scientists turns out to be eerily like the creativity of great artists. The only major difference is the arena in which this creativity operates.

Obviously, creative scientists are not free to create new theoretical worlds at will. They must remain cognizant of previous experimental results, and they must produce ideas that can be tested. And they very often come up with appealing ideas that do not inspire the certainty that motivated Galileo and Einstein. For example, in his book, *A Brief History of Time,* the famous British physicist Stephen Hawking expounded the idea that our universe may have had no beginning in time. According to his theory, at very early times, the dimension of time has the properties of a spatial dimension. At the beginning, Hawking says, there were really only four dimensions of space. Time only acquired an independent character later on.

And how does Hawking know that this is true? He doesn't. I'll be elaborating upon this point later. At the moment, however, it would be better not to interrupt my argument, and to return to the more familiar ideas of Galileo and his predecessors, and of Einstein.

According to Plato, the motions of celestial bodies were as perfect as their Creator could make them. Since the circle was the most perfect geometrical figure, it followed that the sun and the planets must move in circular orbits around a stationary Earth, which was then thought to be the center of the universe. Furthermore, it was obvious that they had to move at constant velocities. A less perfect arrangement was simply inconceivable.

It soon became apparent that there was something wrong with this view. It was obvious even to the naked eye of astronomers from ancient Greece that the velocities of the planets, as seen from the earth, did vary. In fact, at times, some of the planets exhibited retrograde motion; they seemed to move backward in their orbits.

Today this apparent backward motion is easy to explain. Knowing that the sun, and not the earth, is the center of the solar system, we view matters in a somewhat different light. For example, there are times when the earth and Mars are on the same side of the sun. Since the earth moves more rapidly than Mars, and since it has a smaller orbit, there will be times when it catches up with Mars, and passes it, just as a runner on an inner track may pass one who has a lane that is farther out when they round a curve.

The first attempt to explain why the planets moved about in such an irregular way was made by Plato's pupil Eudoxos during the fourth century B.C. According to Eudoxos, the heavens were made up of a system of transparent, interconnected spheres. The outermost sphere carried the stars around the earth. Complicated systems of inner spheres accounted for the motion of the planets. Jupiter, for example, was embedded in a sphere that interacted with three others. Its apparent irregular path in the sky was actually a combination of four different circular motions. There were some twenty-six spheres in all.

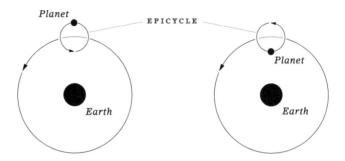

FIG. 1: *Epicycles. The Ptolemaic system was based on the assumption that the sun, moon, and planets all revolved around the earth. As a result, the orbits of the planets could not be assumed to be circles; this was not consistent with observations. A number of different techniques were used to resolve the discrepancy. The most commonly used was the epicycle. Here, the earth is at the center and one of the planets revolves around it. The planet has been placed on a small circle called an epicycle, which itself revolved around the earth. When the planet is on the lower side of the small circle, it appears to be moving backwards.*

The system was further refined by Aristotle, who increased the number of spheres to fifty-five. But Aristotle's system was still incapable of explaining all the observed facts. If the universe was made up of geocentric spheres, then it seemed to follow that the planets must always remain at about the same distance from Earth. However, the planets were observed to vary in brightness, which seemed to imply that the planets were sometimes closer to Earth, and sometimes father away.

So the Greek astronomers and mathematicians devised a new theory to explain the motion of the planets around the earth. They replaced the idea of interlocked spheres with a system of deferents and epicycles. The deferents were earth-centered circles, and epicycles were smaller circles whose centers were on the deferents. The planets revolved, not around the earth, but around points in space that were themselves moving around the earth. The planets were attached to the epicycles. Thus their motion, as seen from the earth, did not appear to be circular. Since they moved on epicycles, their motion appeared to be a series of loops. Sometimes they could loop backwards for short periods of time. Thus the phenomenon of retrograde motion was explained. Since only circles were used, it was possible to avoid contradicting Plato's dictum that only uniform circular motion was possible.

It was an ingenious system, but it still didn't quite work. Discrepencies between theory and observation remained. The problem was finally solved by the Alexandrian astronomer Ptolemy in the second century A.D. He accomplished this by adding more "wheels and pulleys" to an already-complicated theory. Or at least that is our view of the matter. In the eyes of Ptolemy's contemporaries, however, he had devised an admirable mathematical system. In fact, Ptolemy's book on his astronomical work, originally titled *He mathematike syntaxis (The Mathematical Collection)* eventually became known as *Ho megas astronomos (The Great Astronomer)*. During the ninth century, Arab astronomers referred to it as "The Greatest," and it is still known by the Arabic term *Almagest*[1] today.

Ptolemy solved the problem of the discrepencies between astronomical theory and observation by introducing a new concept, that of the *equant*. Since I don't want to bore you with a lot of technical details, I'll confine myself to saying that the equant was a point that was displaced from the earth and that the deferent and epicycles revolved around it. Since even this sounds somewhat technical, I'll try to simplify matters a bit. The deferent was something similar to what we might call an orbit today. But these orbits were not centered on the earth. Furthermore, the planets did not stay fixed on their orbits, but moved around epicycles that were attached to them.

To the modern eye, it looks like a patched-together system. But during ancient times—and in the West after Greek science and philosophy had been assimilated—this didn't seem to make much difference. The philosophers ignored the details of mathematical astronomy, which they were not trained to understand, and continued to teach the doctrine of crystalline spheres. Meanwhile, the astronomers had a theory that allowed them to predict the apparent motion of the planets with reasonable accuracy.

Of course there were some who questioned whether the Ptolemaic theory could really be an accurate representation of reality. One of them was Alfonso X, king of Castille and Leon from 1252 to 1284. Called "Alfonso the Wise," he was already known as a scholar before he became king. After he assumed the throne, he filled his court with scholars, gave large gifts to friends, and engaged in foreign intrigue. All this was expensive, and the taxes that Alfonso imposed were one of the causes of a revolt that led to his downfall in 1284. As a scholar, Alfonso was naturally familiar with Ptolemy's theory. He is reported to have remarked that, if the Almighty had only consulted him before embarking on the Creation, he could have suggested something simpler. But, unlike Alfonso, most scholars simply brushed the question of the reality underlying Ptolemy's theory aside. They simply did not view things in the way that a modern scientist would. If the Ptolemaic system worked, that was all that was required.

COPERNICUS, KEPLER, AND GALILEO

The only problem was that the Ptolemaic system *didn't* quite work. As greater quantities of astronomical data accumulated, it began to be apparent that Ptolemy's theory didn't adequately explain the motions of the planets. New discrepancies appeared. New attempts were made to patch the theory together. However, none of them were completely successful. By the sixteenth century, a number of astronomical systems were in use. But none of them really worked. It is revealing that when the Polish astronomer Copernicus was asked to advise the Church on the matter of calendar reform early in the century, he suggested that the project be postponed. Although only the motions of the sun and moon need to be understood to construct a calendar, Copernicus apparently felt that astronomical knowledge was too incomplete even to describe the motions of these two bodies to the necessary degree of accuracy.

Copernicus eventually set out to construct an astronomical system of his own, one in which the sun, and not the earth, was the center of the solar system. His book *De revolutionbus* appeared in 1543, and Copernicus is supposed to have received the first printed copy when he was on his deathbed. Like many stories of a similar nature, this one may or may not be true. However, its truth or falsity bears little relevance to the fact that Copernicus had set a scientific revolution in motion.

Copernicus' book was highly technical in nature, and virtually unreadable to anyone but astronomers. Nevertheless, it quickly became quite influential. Few of the scholars of the day were willing to accept the idea that the planets really revolved around the sun. However, Copernicus' method did make mathematical calculations easier, and they were willing to accept the idea of a moving earth as a useful mathematical system.

Copernicus' theory did not perfectly describe planetary motion. He assumed that planetary motion was circular, when in reality it is not. As Kepler was later to show, planetary orbits are not circles, but rather elongated curves called ellipses. Copernicus had no way of knowing this. So, although his system did away with the necessity of assuming that the planets sometimes moved backwards in their orbits, he still had to make various *ad hoc* assumptions in order to make theory conform to observations. For example, he assumed that the earth revolved around a point near the sun, not around the sun itself. And he found it necessary to make use of epicycles, just as Ptolemy and his predecessors had. Copernicus' system may have been easier to use than those that were in use when he published his book. But it really did not give more accurate results.

Although Copernicus invented the heliocentric theory, and although Kepler perfected it by introducing elliptical orbits and by deducing laws of planetary motion, it was Galileo who won acceptance for the idea that the earth revolved around the sun. Galileo made no original contributions to the theory. In fact, by insisting that planetary orbits must be circular, not elliptical, he took a step backwards. However, Galileo was the most effective scientific propagandist the world has ever known.

Galileo was a creative scientist. Where his contemporaries attempted to explain natural phenomena according to the doctrines of Aristotle, Galileo insisted upon the importance of experiment. It was his experiments that allowed him to determine the laws governing the behavior of falling bodies. He was also able to determine the paths followed by projectiles. This had important military applications, and Galileo followed up on his theoretical work by designing instruments to determine the proper elevation of cannons when they were aimed at targets a certain distance away.

The story that Galileo dropped weights from the Leaning Tower of Pisa in order to show that a heavy weight and a lighter weight would reach the ground at the same time, by the way, is almost certainly false. There is no mention of the experiment in Galileo's writings, and no contemporary accounts of it. The story makes its first appearance in the writing of one of Galileo's disciples that appeared some years after his master was dead. However, Galileo did invent ingenious *thought experiments* in order to show that the only reasonable conclusion that one could reach was that two falling bodies of different weights would fall at the same rate.

Galileo was the first scientist to have the idea of using a telescope to examine the night sky. In 1609, after hearing that a "certain Dutchman"[2] had invented an instrument that magnified the images of distant objects, Galileo constructed a telescope of his own. His first telescope was an eight-power instrument. This was followed by one that produced a magnification of about twenty, and then by a thirty-power telescope. Using his telescopes to study celestial bodies, Galileo discovered that there were mountains on the moon and dark spots on the sun, and that Venus exhibited phases similar to that of the moon. He also discovered four of the moons of Jupiter.

Galileo was not a professional astronomer, as Kepler was. Or to put it another way, he was not an astrologer. In Galileo's day, no distinction was made between astronomy and astrology, and the casting of horoscopes was the main use of the former. In fact, astrology was then considered to be an important part of a medical education. A physician had to know astrology in order to determine the proper times to administer his medicines. As a professor of mathematics at the University of Padua, Galileo was required to teach mathematical techniques used in astrology. However, as an astronomer, he was an amatuer.

Galileo made no attempt to use his telescopic observations to test Copernicus' theory. In his time, there was no way that this could have been done. However, the results that he obtained were striking. For example, he discovered that the moon had an irregular surface; it was not a perfect sphere, as Aristotle had taught. Galileo found spots on the sun. Obviously it was not perfect either. And his discovery of the moons of Jupiter showed that there were at least some celestial bodies that did not revolve around the earth.

Galileo made great use of his findings in his book *Dialogue Concerning the Two Chief World Systems.* The two systems were, of course, the Copernican and the Ptolemaic. Galileo could not prove that the Copernican theory was true, but he at least made it seem plausible. He did this partly by demolishing some of the arguments against a moving earth that were common in his day. He argued, for example, that a rotating earth could not cause perpetual winds blowing in the opposite direction. The air was carried along with the moving earth. This was analogous to the fact that a heavy object dropped from a mast of a ship did not drift backwards as the ship moved through the ocean. Its inertia in the forward direction caused it to drop directly to a point below it on the deck. One argument was piled on top of another. The book concluded with Galileo's clincher, his incorrect theory of ocean tides.

In a way, Galileo's conception of a sun-centered solar system represented a step backward. Thinking that the ellipse was too ugly a figure to be the basis of planetary motion, he insisted that the planetary orbits were circles. Galileo's status as an amatuer astronomer allowed him to do this. He never had to labor to reconcile theory with astronomical observations the way that Kepler did.

Nevertheless, it was Galileo, not Kepler, who did the most to gain acceptance for Copernicus' ideas. He had a knack for expressing his ideas clearly when he wrote; this made his writing seem all the more persuasive. And, as we all know, the Church forced Galileo to recant his ideas, and placed his book upon the Index. This ensured its popularity, especially outside of Italy. Everyone wants to read a banned book.

But what caused Galileo to repudiate the Ptolemaic theory and to embrace the idea of a sun-centered solar system in the first place? We will never know the answer to this question with absolute certainty. Galileo's writings tell us nothing about the genesis of his ideas, he only argues for their acceptance. Autobiography was not the fashion in his day, at least not among scientists.

However, it is not difficult to guess Galileo's motivations. He obviously considered the Ptolemaic system too complicated to be true. In this he was not alone. Few of the astronomers of the day considered the system to be an accurate representation of reality. Though most continued to believe that the earth was the center of the solar system, astronomical theories were considered to be nothing more than mathematical methods of predicting the positions of the planets. What made Galileo unique was the fact that he was rebellious enough to reject the prevailing Aristotelean doctrine that the earth was the center of the universe, and astute enough to see that the Copernican system possessed an internal logic that was absent from its competitor. Though he spoke of the "two chief world systems" in the title of his book, there were really not any others. Either the earth revolved around the sun, or it didn't. Astronomers had attempted to improve upon Ptolemy's theory for more than a millennium, and had succeeded only in producing a big muddle. Acceptance of the simpler—simpler in concept if not in mathematical detail—Copernican theory made everything clear.

When Isaac Newton discovered his law of universal gravitation sometime between 1664 and 1666, the task of devising an adequate theory of motion in the solar system was completed. In particular, Newton showed that if gravity could be described by an inverse-square law, then it was possible to prove mathematically that planetary orbits had to be elliptical, as Kepler had found. Newton built upon Galileo's studies of the motion near the surface of the earth to formulate his three laws of motion. Together with his law of gravity, this allowed him to describe the behavior of all moving bodies, from a falling apple (the story that Newton hit upon his law of gravitation after watching an apple fall from a tree is probably not true either) to the moon and the planets.

Newton did not encounter the opposition that Galileo had. The latter had prepared the way. By the time Newton's law of universal gravitation was promulgated, the idea that the earth moved around the sun was a familiar one. Newton's theories won immediate acceptance, at least in England, and he became the most famous scientist—or perhaps I should say *natural philosopher*, since the word *scientist* was not used in those days—of his time.

Newton's work had a profound impact upon contemporary thought. It even altered the world views embraced by society at large. For example, at the beginning of the nineteenth century, comets were thought to be ominous portents and the validity of astrology was widely accepted. At the end of the century comets were considered to be nothing more than celestial bodies that were subject to the same laws as the moon and the planets. By this time, belief in astrology had become practically nonexistent among the educated classes. The idea that the planets exterted mysterious influences upon human lives seemed inconsistent with the new scientific world view.

And finally, in 1851, Foucault was able to find a way to demonstrate experimentally that the earth actually did rotate on its axis.

"THE THEORY IS CORRECT"

Much more is known about the genesis of Einstein's ideas than those of Galileo. Einstein frequently wrote and spoke about the steps that led him to the discovery of his relativity theories. Apparently he began thinking about some of the problems while he was still an adolescent. For example, at one point, the young Einstein tried to imagine what it would be like to follow a light wave at the speed of light. He found the pictures that this created in his mind to be somewhat paradoxical. The paradoxes were finally removed when, as an adult, he formulated his special theory of relativity, a theory that described the behavior of bodies that were traveling at velocities approaching that of light.

Einstein's descriptions of his thought processes tell us that he thought along lines similar to those that I have surmised were present in the mind of Galileo. Einstein often emphasized the fact that he considered the inner logic and clarity of a theory to be more important than experimental confirmation. For example, his general theory of relativity—his theory of gravitation—predicted that a ray of light that grazed the surface of the sun would be deflected by a certain amount. In 1919, an expedition of British scientists traveled to Africa to observe the sun during an eclipse, and reported that Einstein's predictions had been confirmed.

When the news arrived in Germany, one of Einstein's students, Ilse Rosenthal-Schneider, noticed that he seemed unmoved by the fact that his theory had been confirmed. Consequently she asked him why he didn't seem to be as excited as she was. "But I knew that the theory is correct," Einstein replied. When Rosenthal-Schneider asked him how he would have reacted if the experimental results had been unfavorable, he said, "Then I would have been sorry for the dear Lord—the theory is correct."

In reality the observations, made by the British astronomer Arthur Eddington and his colleagues, were not so very conclusive. There was a high margin of error, and it was not absolutely necessary to conclude that Einstein's general theory had passed an important test. Yet the scientists of the day, at least those who understood what Einstein had done, generally viewed Eddington's results as a confirmation. Like Galileo when he pondered the Copernican theory, they could not believe that so clear and logical a formulation could be wrong.

Science progresses much more rapidly today than it did in the time of Galileo and Newton. Thus physicists did not have to wait two centuries before accurate experimental tests of general relativity were made. During the 1960s physicists performed numerous different kinds of experiments that verified the predictions of Einstein's theory to a high degree of accuracy. And of course, when the experiments were begun, few physicists had any doubts about the outcome. By the 1960s, general relativity had been almost universally accepted for some time.

Einstein's intuitions were not infallible. For example, during the 1930s some physicists began to speculate about the possible existence of the bodies we now call black holes. A black hole is an object, formed from the remnants of a dead star, that is so condensed that nothing that falls within its gravitation clutches can ever escape. The term *black hole* is a reference to the fact that not even light can escape from it.

Einstein could not accept the idea that so bizarre an object could actually exist, and in 1939 he published a paper that purported to prove that black holes were impossible. And of course his arguments were incorrect. His mathematics was accurate enough. But he had begun with questionable assumptions. Today we know that black holes are quite common in our universe. Naturally it is not possible to travel through space to observe them at close range. However, astronomers have discovered numerous objects that could be nothing else. Though a black hole cannot not be seen, it exerts gravitational forces on neighboring objects that causes behavior that can be observed. This has revealed the existence of invisible bodies that are massive and almost inconceivably condensed.

Although Einstein may have sometimes been wrong when he looked at the details, his conception of the basic structure of the universe has turned out to be correct. To be sure, relativity, like all theories, has its limits. In particular, general relativity cannot describe the behavior of matter in the limit where quantum effects become important. For example, one can use Einstein's theory to describe the formation of a black hole. But if all of the matter inside the hole falls to its center, as Einstein's theory says it should, then a state of infinite density would be produced. Astrophysicists think that quantum effects would intervene before this happens, but they don't know what these effects would be. In the limit of extremely high density, the theory simply breaks down.

On the other hand, there are no significant problems associated with using general relativity to describe the structure of the universe as a whole. And the reason that we have such a theory is not that Einstein sought ideas that were falsifiable. On the contrary, he made use of his great imagination to create pictures of reality that were so imposing and so logical that it was virtually impossible to doubt them.

QUANTUM MECHANICS

One should always be wary of generalizations. Einstein's theories generally created pictures of physical reality that could (at least by physicists) easily be visualized. A great deal of their appeal derived from the fact that they created very clear cut models of the physical world. But this has not always been the case. When the German physicist Werner Heisenberg discovered quantum mechanics in 1925, he did not create any new picture of subatomic reality at all. Heisenberg's theory used a kind of mathematics, called *matrix mechanics*, which was unfamiliar to most physicists (but had long been known to mathematicians), to relate observable quantities, such as wavelengths of light, to one another. Heisenberg was concerned only with what could be seen in the laboratory, not in whatever microscopic reality there might be lying behind the observations.

But the development of the theory did not stop there. In 1926, the Austrian physicist Erwin Schrödinger independently developed his own theory of the behavior of subatomic particles. He called his theory *wave mechanics* because particles were viewed as being made up of bundles of waves. Though both theories seemed equally workable in the sense that they seemed to explain the phenomena that scientists observed in the laboratory, neither scientist was able to appreciate what the other had done. Each described the other's theory in derogatory terms.

I'm sure you can guess what happened next. In 1926, the German physicist Max Born proved that the Heisenberg and Schrödinger formulations were mathematically equivalent, and the two scientists are now thought of as the cofounders of quantum mechanics.

But even after Born published his proof, it was not clear exactly what kind of picture of subatomic reality had been created. To be sure, Schrödinger spoke of waves, but it was not clear precisely what it was that was *waving*. Born was later able to prove that the height of Schrödinger's waves was related to the probability that a particle would be found at some particular point in space. But this did not exactly clear matters up. In fact, the arguments about the proper interpretation of quantum mechanics continue to this day.

The fact that such arguments are conducted should not be allowed to obscure the fact that quantum mechanics is an extremely accurate theory. It is possible to use it to make predictions that have been confirmed by experiment to an accuracy greater than anything else in physics. At first, only the statistical predictions of the theory could be tested. For example, the light emitted by the particles that made up a gas could be measured and compared to theoretical calculations. These results were statistical because a sample of a gas generally consists of many billions of atoms, and the light has a character that represents a kind of statistical average.

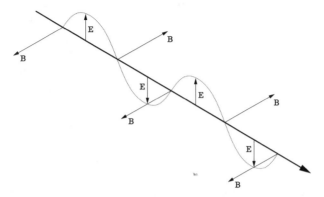

FIG. 2: *Light as an electromagnetic wave. Light and other kinds of radiation are made up of oscillating electric and magnetic fields. Here* E *represents the electric field and* B *(the symbol normally used by physicists) the magnetic field.* B *is perpendicular to* E. *The ray of light is traveling to the right. The fine line is a sine wave that shows the oscillations of* E. *When Einstein was still an adolescent, he wondered what an observer who was traveling at the speed of light would see, and concluded that he would observe stationary electric and magnetic fields at right angles to one another. He found this paradoxical because such stationary fields are not observed in nature.*

But today it is possible to test quantum mechanical predictions about the behavior of single particles, and the theory passes these tests with flying colors. For example, it has been shown that a neutron can indeed move along two paths at the same time, as the theory predicts, and that an atom can occupy two positions at once.

Unlike the heliocentric system of Copernicus and Einstein's theories of relativity, which appeared to be clear and logical from the very first, quantum mechanics has always seemed to have an illogical, or at least very strange, character. One can say that we should not expect objects in the subatomic world to behave in the same manner as macroscopic objects. And perhaps the fact that quantum mechanics is a logically and mathematically consistent theory should be enough for us. However, its success shows us that there can be a lot more to discovering a new theory than creating a vivid mental picture. Sometimes the world embodies a kind of logic that we do not expect.

But in the end, one is forced to conclude that the story of the triumph of quantum mechanics exhibits similarities to those of the acceptance of the Copernican system and of Einstein's theories. Heisenberg and Schrödinger had the same kind of creative vision that we can see in the work of Einstein. The story of quantum mechanics even resembles that of its predecessors in that the crucial experiments that could have falsified it were not performed until long after the theory had gained acceptance. As I mentioned above, it is only today that the predictions of quantum mechanics about the behavior of single particles can really be tested. And of course the physicists who have carried out the tests never dreamed that the theory would be contradicted. It simply explained too much to be wrong.

IMAGINARY TIME

According to Stephen Hawking, the universe had a beginning in imaginary time. I imagine that many of the lay readers of his book, *A Brief History of Time,* must have found this idea a bit confusing. Hawking doesn't make it sufficiently clear that he is using the term *imaginary* in a technical, mathematical sense that is unrelated to the meaning of the word *imaginary* when it is used in ordinary conversation.

Hawking's idea makes use of an extension of the concept of imaginary numbers. An example of an imaginary number is the square root of -4. Obviously the square root cannot be 2 because $2 \times 2 = 4$. It can't be -2 either, because -2×-2 is also equal to 4; the minus signs cancel out. Hence the square root of -4 is said to be imaginary. Today, mathematicians say that the square root of -4 is 2i, where i is a number that has the property that i × i = -1.

The existence of imaginary numbers was first noticed by Hero of Alexandria in the first century A.D., but it wasn't until the nineteenth century that they were widely accepted by mathematicians. Today, imaginary numbers are considered as real as any other number, and complex numbers—combinations of real and imaginary quantities—are widely used in physics, in mathematics, and in engineering. Their use makes certain kinds of calculations easier. If they seem to be abstract quantities, that bothers no one. After all, the number 2 is abstract too. You may run into two people on the street, or eat two oranges, or stay up until two in the morning, but in ordinary life you will never encounter the number two.

One example of the use of imaginary numbers is provided by Schrödinger's wave equation, which is frequently used by physicists who work with quantum mechanics. It turns out that Schrödinger's waves are described by complex numbers. This was one of the things that caused the physicists of the mid-1920s to wonder what it was that was *waving*. But when Born showed that it was only the height of the wave that had any real physical meaning, the problem disappeared. When complex numbers are manipulated mathematically, real numbers often result. This is what happened when Born did calculations involving Schrödinger's waves. He didn't answer the "What is waving?" question, but he did show that the waves were related to quantities that could be measured.

THE TERRORS OF THE INFINITE

Before I describe Hawking's use of imaginary numbers in his account of the origin of the universe, I should probably say something about the problem that he was trying to solve. As most of us know, the universe is expanding. Consequently it must originally have been in a very compressed state. In fact, it can be mathematically proved that, if Einstein's general theory of relativity is correct, the universe must have begun with a state of infinite density. It makes no difference what assumptions one makes about the nature of the expansion. There are theorems that state that, no matter what the universe is doing now, it must originally have been in a state where all the matter in it was compressed into a single, dimensionless, mathematical point.

Now, physicists don't especially like dealing with infinite quantities. There are paradoxes associated with them, and no infinities have ever been observed in nature. Consequently, when a theory predicts the existence of an infinite quantity, this is generally taken to be an indication that there is something wrong with the theory.

At first, the conclusion that the mass density of the universe must have orignally been infinite seems to present no problem. As I have pointed out previously there are points at which all theories break down. In particular, Einstein's general theory is no longer applicable when mass densities become very high. Thus there is no reason to believe that the infinites that it predicts were real.

But this doesn't really solve the problem. If the universe didn't begin with a state of infinite density, then exactly how did it begin? Naturally, general relativity is of no help here. It simply can't describe what was happening at the very beginning.

Now quantum mechanics is a theory that is generally applied to the behavior of subatomic particles. However if it is a correct theory, then there was no reason why it could not be applied to the universe as a whole. During the 1980s, Hawking and other theoretical physicists used this idea to create a new field, called quantum cosmology. The best known result to come out of this endeavor was a theory developed by Hawking and the American physicist James

Hartle to explain the origin of the universe. It was the Hawking-Hartle theory that introduced the concept of imaginary time.

As we have seen, imaginary quantities frequently crop up in quantum mechanics. In most cases, they disappear at the end of a calculation, and one is left only with real numbers. But in the Hawking-Hartle theory there is a difference. It is assumed that, at the very beginning, time had an imaginary (remember that this term is being used in the mathematical sense!) character, which it then lost as the early universe evolved.

Now it so happens that a specific meaning can be attached to the idea of imaginary time. Imaginary time resembles a dimension of space. You should not be very surprised by this result. As we all know, time and space are quantities that are very much alike in some respects. Both can be measured, and both imply the concept of distance. For example, we can say that an event took place ten years in the past or that it happened at a place ten miles away. It is not so very unreasonable to conclude that time might take on the character of a space dimension if it becomes imaginary. All that has happened is that one kind of distance is changed into the other.

There is no way of knowing whether imaginary time really once existed, and it is not easy to think of ways in which the theory might be falsified. When I called Hartle to discuss the theory while researching another book, he insisted that the theory could be subjected to observational tests. A universe that began in a certain manner would lead to a universe that had certain characteristics today. However, I suspect that only some physicists would agree with this evaluation. There are probably many theoretical schemes that could produce a universe like ours.

The Hawking-Hartle theory might become widely accepted in time. But at present it is not. For example, the British astrophysicist Michael Rowan-Robinson, who believes that there is a 99 percent chance that the big bang theory gives a correct description of the universe from a time of one second after the big bang, estimates that the imaginary time theory has only a 1 percent chance of turning out to be the "way forward." It may be that Rowan-Robinson's estimate is a bit too conservative. However, the theory is far from being generally accepted.

Naturally Hawking realizes this, and he has referred to the imaginary time idea as a *proposal* rather than a *theory*, or even a *hypothesis*. The difference is significant. In science, a *theory* is something that has been relatively well established. A *hypothesis* is something more tentative. This is reflected in the fact that we speak of Einstein's *theory* of relativity and of Darwin's *theory* of evolution when both have gained virtually universal acceptance among scientists.

The validity of Hawking's proposal is made all the more uncertain by the fact that there exist other plausible scenarios for the creation of the universe[3] that also avoid the assumption of an initial state of infnite density. It appears that Hawking and Hartle have created an imaginary universe in their minds that may or may not bear some resemblance to the universe in which we live.

Hawking is no less a creative scientist than Copernicus, or Galileo, or Einstein. And he has developed other theories that are generally accepted even though they cannot yet be confirmed by any solid scientific evidence. For example, his theory that black holes will eventually explode after a certain period of time is now an accepted part of astrophysics. No one has ever seen such an explosion. An ordinary black hole would have a lifetime many orders of magnitude greater than the age of the universe, and the shorter-lived *mini black holes* that Hawking postulates might have been created in the big bang have not been observed. However, few doubt Hawking's conclusions.

It appears that the creative scientific imagination can

work in a number of different ways. When Galileo insisted that the earth moved around the sun, and when Einstein proposed his theories of relativity, there appeared to be a certain inevitability about their conclusions. To scientists who took the trouble to understand their work, it seemed virtually impossible that they could be wrong. On the other hand, when Hawking speaks of imaginary time, no such feeling of inevitability seems to be present. As far as we know, the universe that he and Hartle have created exists only within their minds.

TWO QUESTIONS

It appears that a preliminary look at the workings of the scientific imagination has raised a number of different questions: How is it possible that correct theories can come to be accepted long before there is any evidence to support them? How could the contemporaries of Galileo, Newton, and Einstein be so sure that the theories they believed in were true? Secondly, what, exactly, is the difference between developing a theory that has a very good chance to be true and creating a universe, such as that of Hawking and Hartle, that may exist only in the mind?

I am not sure that I can answer these questions in full. However, I think you will agree that the examples that I have given so far suggest that it would be worthwhile to look at the workings of the scientific imagination in more detail. Even if we reach no final conclusions, it should at least become apparent that the workings of the creative mind are not so very different in science than they are in the arts.

NOTES

[1] This isn't really an Arabic word. It comes from a combination of the Greek superlative *megiste* and the Arabic definite article *al*.

[2] The German-Dutch lens grinder Hans Lippershey.

[3] Some of these are discussed in my book *Cosmic Questions* (Wiley, 1993).

CHAPTER 2

HOW TO TELL WHAT IS SCIENCE
FROM WHAT ISN'T SCIENCE

There exists little or no evidence supporting the Hartle-Hawking proposal about the origin of the universe. There exist a number of other theories that are equally plausible,[1] and until much more scientific research is done, accepting one hypothesis or another is a matter of taste. For that matter, it would not be unreasonable to maintain an attitude of skepticism concerning all these theories. In fact, there is more evidence for astrology than there is for Hartle and Hawking's idea. For example, studies have been performed that supposedly show correlations between date of birth and the occupation that an individual later adopts. To be sure, these studies are controversial, they don't seem to conform to standard astrological ideas, and the most comprehensive study of astrology that has been carried out, one conducted by Shawn Carlson, a researcher at the University of California's Lawrence Berkeley Laboratory, seemed to show that the *best* astrologers could not perform at a level better than chance. But isn't some evidence better than nothing?

Nevertheless, scientists are virtually unanimous in regarding astrology as pseudoscience, while they generally consider the Hartle-Hawking proposal to be a legitimate scientific idea. This brings up the question of exactly what the difference is between scientific ideas and those that are psuedoscience. Popper's theory is of no help here. Although Popper thought that astrology could not be falsified, the contrary seems to be the case. And, for the foreseeable future, the Hartle-Hawking proposal is not very likely to satisfy his criterion of falsifiability. It seems that, if we really want to claim it is possible to tell science from what isn't science, we shall have to look elsewhere.

Thomas Kuhn's book, *The Structure of Scientific Revolutions*, which was published in 1962, was nearly as influential as Popper's book. Kuhn, a historian of science at Princeton University, discussed scientific paradigms, and the manner in which an old paradigm is replaced by new ideas. Kuhn was not primarily interested in distinguishing between science and pseudoscience. However, he did claim that science was a problem-solving activity, whereas pseudoscience was not. Kuhn's criterion does seem to work in the case of astrology, but I think that it fails elsewhere. Investigators of UFO phenomena and crop circles certainly seem to be trying to solve puzzles. The argument that most scientists have with them is that they are dealing with problems that don't exist. For example, there is no real evidence that would indicate that the earth is being visited by extraterrestrial craft, and no artifact of extraterrestrial origin has ever been found. If you doubt the importance of the latter, consider the fact that we have left numerous artifacts on the moon. The signs of our presence there are unmistakable. Similarly, at least some crop circles were created by hoaxers. The simplest explanation for the others is they were made in a similar manner.

At this point I should probably issue a disclaimer. I am not a philosopher of science, and it is not my intention to improve on the criteria that were invented by Popper and Kuhn. My subject here is the scientific imagination. However it will be necessary to say a bit about what is not science. The scientific imagination would be hard to describe if we didn't know what we meant by the word *scientific*.

This problem doesn't seem to exist in the world of art. To be sure, there is a lot of bad art in the world, some of it created by great artists.[2] But we generally don't deny that it is art, however banal the conception may have been, however clumsy the execution.

WORLDS IN COLLISION

I promise to return to the subject of science shortly. However, I don't think it would do any harm to give another example of a pseudoscientific theory, this time in more detail. Immanuel Velikovsky's ideas are not so fashionable as they once were, although there is still some interest in his book, *Worlds in Collision*, which was originally published in 1950. According to Velikovsky, Venus had its origin from a comet that was expelled by the planet Jupiter around the middle of the second millennium B.C. Venus then bounded around the solar system, passing near the earth on several occasions. Finally, an encounter with Mars caused it to assume the nearly circular orbit that it has today. The near-collisions with the earth were supposedly the cause of certain catastrophic events described in the Old Testament and by various ancient myths. It was mythology, Velikovsky said, that provided clues to the origin of Venus. It so happens that, according to one myth, Athena was born from the brow of Zeus. In order to assist in this rather difficult labor, Hermes, who was a physician as well as the god of thieves, split open Zeus' forehead with a wedge. Athena then sprang forth, wearing full armor.

Now it is usually Aphrodite, not Athena, who is identified with the planet Venus. But this didn't trouble Velikovsky, who claimed that there were reasons for believing that Athena originally represented Venus, while Aphrodite was the goddess of the moon. The ensuing near-collision of Venus with the earth, Velikovsky went on, was responsible for the plagues that afflicted Egypt when the pharaoh would not allow the Israelites to leave. Venus was also the cause of the parting of the Red Sea and of the manna that fell in the wilderness.

We might object that Velikovsky had a tendency to take myth a little too seriously. Indeed, this point was made by his critics at the time. However, one of Velikovsky's predictions was confirmed when Soviet space vehicles entered the atmosphere of Venus during the late 1960s. The scientific data that they obtained showed that the surface and atmosphere of Venus were very hot, just as Velikovsky had said. On the other hand, scientists had previously believed that Venus was relatively cool.

So, when confronted by the new evidence in support of Velikovsky's ideas, did scientists decide that they must take the theory seriously? Of course not. They considered it a crackpot theory before the evidence about Venus was obtained, and they consider it a crackpot theory today. As it turned out, they were vindicated. The confirmation of Velikovsky's prediction turned out not to be very good after all. In the first place, scientific theories are generally expected to yield quantitative predictions. Velikovsky had said that Venus was hot, but he hadn't specified exactly how hot it should be. According to Velikovsky's theory, the planet should be cooling off. It isn't. Finally, during the 1970s it was established that Venus was hot, not because it had once been a comet, but because it had experienced a runaway greenhouse effect.

Some of Velikovsky's other predictions failed miserably. He had stated, for example, that the clouds of Venus were made of hydrocarbons. But in 1973, it was found that the clouds were actually composed of sulfuric acid vapor. The atmosphere of Venus is about 93 percent carbon dioxide. Nitrogen, water vapor, and carbon monoxide are also present, but hydrocarbons are not.

Velikovsky had a special reason for proposing that hydrocarbons existed on Venus. These were supposedly the cause of the manna that fell in the wilderness to nourish the Israelites after they fled Egypt. The only problem with this hypothesis is that hydrocarbons are not exactly edible. The simplest hydrocarbon is methane, the gas we use to cook with. More complex hydrocarbons are the components of crude oil. When petroleum is refined, one obtains a solid residue that is also composed primarily of hydrocarbons. It is called asphalt. Possibly Velikovsky enjoyed eating pieces of roadway. But I certainly don't, and most likely you don't either. Or perhaps he simply didn't know the difference between hydrocarbons and carbohydrates.

When the theory is examined in more detail, further problems appear. Velikovsky claimed that Venus was ejected from Jupiter. But the energy required to expel a body of this size would be greater than that radiated by the sun during the course of a year. Velikovsky never explained where this energy came from. He never explained what the forces were that supposedly kept the earth and Venus in close proximity to one another for a period of months, and he didn't adequately explain what prevented them from colliding. According to Velikovsky, the impact was cushioned by the magnetic fields of the two planets. But the earth has a magnetic field that is very weak, one that cannot even move a compass needle unless the needle is very delicately suspended. And Venus turns out to have no measurable magnetic field at all. Even if we suppose that something was going on that prevented the earth and Venus from colliding, it is still not clear how they could have survived the encounter. Tidal forces would have ripped both planets apart.

If one wants to accept Velikovsky's theory, then it is necessary to ignore long-standing principles in physics, chemistry, astronomy, and biology. After all, the theory postulates the existence of unknown sources of energy than can cause a planet-sized object to be ejected from another. It depends on tidal forces that fail to act, on strange forces that can keep planets together for months, and then allow them to drift apart, on magnetic fields that become mysteriously strong, and on the edibility of petroleum derivatives. To accept it, it is necessary to throw out or to disregard numerous scientific principles that have long been established.

And that is the problem. Velikovsky's theory explains no

observed natural phenomena, and accepting it would force us to come to the conclusion that much of the scientific knowledge that has been laboriously built up over a period of centuries is simply wrong. In fact, one could reasonably characterize it, not as pseudoscience, but as antiscience.

Galileo had no more facts to support his contention that the Copernican theory must be correct than Velikovsky had. But Galileo was astute enough to realize that, once one adopted the Copernican system, everything seemed to hang together. At the time, few of the astronomers who used the competing Ptolemaic theory really believed that it provided an accurate representation of reality. According to their way of thinking, it was simply a way of *saving the appearances*, of devising mathematical methods that would allow them to predict planetary positions with some degree of accuracy. To make things worse, most of the astronomical systems then in use gave results that were about as accurate as those obtained from any other.

The Copernican system had its defects. But, for the first time, scientists had a theory that explained astronomical phenomena in an intuitive way. The theory provided no explanation of why the earth should go around the sun. Newton would work that out later. But it did provide a way of looking at things that made sense. Galileo believed that, given a choice between the Ptolemaic and Copernican systems, the only reasonable thing that one could do was to conclude that only the latter must be correct.

RELATIVITY

When Einstein published papers on his special theory of relativity in 1905, many scientists found his ideas to be very bizarre. Yet none of them claimed that Einstein had created a pseudoscientific theory. Contrary to popular belief, Einstein did not overthrow any previously accepted ideas. In fact, his theory successfully explained some long-standing scientific puzzles. For example, at the time, physicists had a theory of electricity and magnetism, that of the Scottish physicist James Clerk Maxwell, which was considered to be well established. Not only did it explain the behavior of magnets and their interaction with electrical currents, it also allowed scientists to understand the nature of light. Light, physicists believed, was a wave phenomenon; the waves were made up of oscillating electric and magnetic fields. The theory had been confirmed over and over again by experiment.

Nevertheless there were difficulties. For example, if a magnet is moved through a loop of wire, an electrical current will be induced. The same thing happens if the magnet is stationary and the wire is moved over the magnet. This was all very reasonable. Physicists had known since the time of Galileo that relative motion was the only thing that mattered. If I am struck by a bullet moving at a high velocity, the effects will be exactly the same as they would be if the bullet were stationary and I were moving rapidly. And if two automobiles with a relative velocity of 100 miles per hours collide with one another, it makes no difference how fast either one was moving. Each will sustain the same amount of damage in any case.

When Einstein published his first paper on relativity, the title that he gave it hardly sounded earth-shattering. He called it "On the Electrodynamics of Moving Bodies." He was able to show that, if his theory was accepted, this old problem was finally cleared up. In fact, Einstein often emphasized the fact that special relativity had been devised to explain known experimental facts. If some of the conclusions that he reached, for example that rapidly moving objects seem to contract in the direction of their motion while simultaneously increasing in mass, seemed strange, it was only a consequence of the fact that the theory brought new order to certain areas of physics.

Many people believe that Einstein somehow overthrew

[175]

Newton's laws of motion and of gravitation. Nothing could be further from the truth. Newton's laws can be derived from the equations of relativity if one assumes that the bodies under consideration move at velocities that are small compared to the speed of light. Newton's law of gravitation turns out to be a special case of Einstein's general theory of relativity; it is valid whenever gravitational fields are not too intense. In fact it is Newton's law, not Einstein's, that scientists use in most cases today. For example, it would be crazy to use Einstein's equations (which can get very complicated) to compute the path of a space vehicle. The differences between the predictions of Einstein's theory and Newton's are simply too small to be measured. It only becomes necessary to use Einstein's law when gravitational fields become very strong, for example near the surface of a black hole.

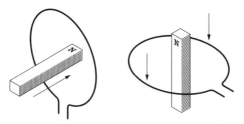

FIG. 3: *An electromagnetic paradox. When a magnet is moved through a loop of wire, an electrical current is set up in the wire. The same current is set up as the wire is moved and the magnet remains stationary. But the classical laws of electricity and magnetism describe the two cases differently. In the first case, there is a changing magnetic field (because the magnet moves). In the second case, the magnetic field remains the same. Einstein resolved this paradox with his special theory of relativity.*

Einstein's theories were accepted because they did not contradict what had previously been known and also because they cleared up anomalies that had previously been somewhat annoying. I have already made reference to one of these, that of the induction of a current in a wire. Another has to do with the orbit of Mercury, which is not quite elliptical as Newton's law says it should be. Successive orbits do not return it to the same points in space. The orbit slowly swivels around the sun instead. This phenomenon has been known for some time. During the early twentieth century many astronomers believed that it was caused by a planet inside the orbit of Mercury. This hypothetical planet was even given a name, Vulcan, and numerous attempts were made to find it. Naturally these were doomed to failure. Einstein showed that the orbit of Mercury (which is the closest planet to the sun, and which therefore experiences the strongest gravitational forces) was just as it should be.

A good scientific theory ties up scientific knowledge in a pleasing, harmonious way. It may remove anomalies that have troubled scientists for years. And it typically predicts new phenomena that have not yet been observed. Modern high-energy particle physics provides a good example of this. The existence of most of the known subatomic particles was predicted by theory before they were observed in experiments. Quarks, the components of protons and neutrons—and of numerous more exotic particles as well—were originally a purely theoretical concept. Their existence was confirmed years after the idea was proposed.

BAD SCIENCE

Just because an idea is *scientific*, it doesn't necessarily follow that it is good science. One of the classic examples was the discovery of N rays by the distinguished French physicist René Blondlot in 1903. If you have never heard of N rays, you can probably be forgiven. N rays don't exist. But Blondlot, who was a member of the French Academy of Sciences, and anything but a crackpot, thought otherwise.

After X rays were discovered in 1895, Blondlot began

performing experiments in an attempt to answer a question that had been puzzling physicists: Were X rays composed of subatomic particles, or were they a form of electromagnetic radiation like radio waves and like light? During the course of his experiments, Blondlot discovered certain puzzling electrical phenomena. At first he thought that X rays were the cause. But further experimentation proved that this was impossible. At this point, Blondlot made an intuitive leap. It was not so great a leap as those of Galileo or of Einstein. But it was an act of creative imagination nevertheless. If X rays were not causing the phenomena he observed, then some other kind of radiation must be. He gave this unknown radiation the name *N rays*.

Shortly after Blondlot published his results, other scientists began to build upon his work. It was found that wood, paper, and thin sheets of such metals as tin, silver, and gold were transparent to N rays, but that they could not pass through such substances as water or rock salt. Shortly thereafter it was discovered that N rays were emitted by the human body, and by corpses as well. This led to suggestions concerning possible medical uses of the new kind of radiation. There was apparently no reason why N rays could not be used to examine internal organs.

Nevertheless there were doubts. Some experimenters found that they were unable to reproduce the results that had been reported by Blondlot and other scientists. When they tried to produce and detect N rays in their own laboratories, they observed nothing. Soon some of them began to entertain doubts about the reality of this new kind of radiation.

The American physicist Robert Williams Wood was one of these skeptics. But he did not confine himself to writing about the matter. In 1905 he visited Blondlot's laboratory and found that he could not see the effects that Blondlot claimed to be observing (in those days, scientists depended much more on visual observations than they do today). So when Blondlot was not looking, he made some alterations in the setup of Blondlot's apparatus. The changes that he made should have made it impossible to observe N rays. But Blondlot continued to see their effects anyway.

The story should have ended there, but it didn't. Even after Wood demonstrated that N rays were an illusion, many French scientists continued to accept Blondlot's results. Some even claimed that only French scientists had the visual sensitivity to see the phenomena that N rays produced. The senses of Anglo-Saxon scientists, they said, had been dulled by exposure to English fog, while those of German researchers had been blunted by excessive consumption of beer. It was only when Blondlot refused to participate in a test for the existence of N rays that had been proposed by the French journal *Revue scientifique* that interest in the topic finally waned.

Blondlot's research on N rays may have been bad science. But it was science nevertheless. At the time, both X rays and the phenomenon of radioactivity had recently been discovered. There was no reason why other previously unknown kinds of radiation might not exist in nature. To be sure, Blondlot's research depended on observations that involved a certain element of subjectivity: changes in brightness of an electrical discharge. But this kind of thing was really not so uncommon in his day. Early nineteenth-century scientists did not have the kinds of instruments that exist today and visual observations were considered to be reasonably legitimate. To be sure, Blondlot allowed himself to become a victim of his own self-deception. But even Einstein was not immune to that.

Einstein had possessed superb physical intuition that guided him toward the solution of outstanding problems in physics and that led him toward the creation of his theories. It was his intuition that told him that the general theory of relativity *had* to be correct. Nothing else was reasonable. And, in fact, his theories have been confirmed over and over

[179]

again. This didn't always happen during his lifetime; the accurate experimental tests of general relativity came after his death. But, significantly, physicists were convinced of the theory's validity even before these tests were performed.

But sometimes Einstein's intuition led him astray. We have already encountered one example, his "proof" that black holes could not exist. He was also led astray when he attempted to use the general theory of relativity to describe the structure of the universe. Believing that the universe must be static and unchanging, he attempted to describe such a universe mathematically. Unfortunately, he made some elementary mathematical mistakes, which were later corrected by other physicists.

There are analogies to this in the world of art. We often tend to ignore this fact, and quite rightly judge artists by their best work, not by their worst. However, few would claim that Beethoven's overture "Wellington's Victory" is a good piece of music or that Shakespeare's *Titus Andronicus* is anything but a bad play. True, it has been suggested that other authors may have had a hand in the composition of Shakespeare's tragedy. But one of the reasons for believing this is the feeling that Shakespeare could not have written something so awful. There is no documentary evidence of coauthorship.

The idea that it is possible to find parallels between scientific and artistic creation is one that I will return to later, perhaps without reaching any definite conclusions. These two fields of human activity are so different that it is difficult to say exactly *how* they are alike. I am bringing up the question now in order to emphasize the fact that scientific theories are free creations of the human mind. Unlike artistic creations, they must eventually be confirmed by experiment if they are to be taken very seriously. However, it should be clear by now that scientific theories are not generalizations from observed fact. On the contrary, it is theory that determines what experiments should be performed.

[180]

PARAPSYCHOLOGY

Bad science exists because the scientific imagination is anything but infallible. But, like everything else in the world, the boundaries of bad science are somewhat fuzzy. For example, it is not clear whether parapsychology is a pseudoscience, or another example of the scientific imagination gone astray.

Critics of parapsychology often cite that fact that the existence of telepathy, clairvoyance, precognition, and so on has never really been demonstrated. One has to conclude that this is indeed the case. I am thinking here of laboratory studies, not of the supposed parapsychological "powers" of self-proclaimed psychics. Though the latter receive considerable attention in the media, they fall outside the scope of this book. I will confine myself to a discussion of studies that purport to be scientific.

The "science" of parapsychology is an outgrowth of the spiritualist movement that flourished during the latter half of the nineteenth century. Parapsychological phenomena began to be studied in earnest when the Society of Psychical Research was founded in London in 1892. In the United States attempts to establish parapsychology as a science began when J.B. Rhine of Duke University began conducting laboratory experiments in the 1930s. These continued until the early 1960s, when he retired.

Many of the early ESP experiments were conducted under rather lax conditions. Few precautions were taken to prevent deception by the subjects or unconscious errors by the experimenters. When, in response to criticism by orthodox scientists, Rhine tightened up his experimental procedures, the evidence for the existence of ESP became less dramatic. It would not be unreasonable to conclude that, in thirty years of work, Rhine was able to prove nothing. Nor was the field of parapsychology without its scandals. For example, in 1974, it was discovered that Walter J. Levy, Jr., who had succeeded Rhine as director of the parapsychological laboratory at Duke had been guilty of fraud. Three staff members of the laboratory caught him falsifying data from one of his experiments. To his credit, Rhine himself reported and commented upon the scandal. However, the discovery of fraud only acted to cast further doubt upon the validity of what many already considered a *fringe* science.

Nevertheless, experiments in parapsychology continued. Many of them were carried out at the Stanford Research Institute (no connection with Stanford University) in California. But the work again failed to be very convincing. It was at SRI, for example, that scientists tested the supposed powers of the Israeli stage magician and psychic Uri Geller, and reported favorably on his performance.[3] But the results obtained at SRI failed to be very convincing. They were probably less so than those of Rhine, who apparently did proceed with a great deal of integrity, and who made serious efforts to impose experimental controls.

It would be possible to go on at length about the history of parapsychology. Indeed, some writers, such as Martin Gardner, have written about it extensively. However, I am more concerned by the question of why the results that have been obtained in the field have been almost universally rejected by scientists. After all, even though nothing has been conclusively demonstrated, it would not be so unreasonable to attempt to investigate certain kinds of paranormal phenomena further. In fact, this is exactly what parapsychologists attempt to do.

The reason that parapsychology is almost universally rejected by scientists has to do the with the fact that there exists no theory that might explain how telepathy, clairvoyance, and psychokinesis operate. The same is true of precognition with the added difficulty that any believer in precognition is forced to assume that the future can somehow influence the present. If I know what is going to happen tomorrow, I may alter my behavior accordingly.

The rejection does not stem from scientists' reluctance to entertain new ideas. No one who is familiar with the history of modern physics, especially that of the apparently paradoxical field of quantum mechanics[4] could believe that. In fact, the great Danish physicist Niels Bohr is supposed to have once objected to a theory on the grounds that it was "not crazy enough." On the contrary, they reject it because it seems to have no theoretical foundation. Parapsychologists claim that ESP exists, but they cannot say how it operates.

One encounters something similar in the field of medicine. When physicians express doubts about the usefulness of alternative therapies, they do not do so because they are closed minded. In fact, some rather outlandish-seeming treatments have become part of modern medicine. For example, causing a wound to become infested with maggots is an excellent treatment for gangrene. The maggots eat the gangrenous flesh and leave healthy tissue alone.[5] On the other hand, physicians almost universally reject the claims of homeopathy. Homeopathic remedies are prepared using series of dilutions. In many cases, the dilution is so great that not one atom of the supposedly therapeutic substance remains. Homeopathy is rejected partly because of lack of evidence for its value, and partly because claims made for the efficacy of its methods seem so unreasonable.

It is true that some attempts have been made to explain ESP in terms of quantum mechanics. At first this might seem a little odd, since quantum mechanics deals with the behavior of subatomic particles, not with things that we see in our mind's eye. But physicists do not find these attempts to be very convincing. I suspect that the majority of them would agree with Martin Gardner's characterization when he calls them "quack theory."

For better or worse, the reality of extrasensory phenomena is rejected because they cannot be explained in terms of any reasonable theory. This provides yet another example of the primacy of theory—the creations of the human mind—in science. All-embracing theoretical visions can be accepted long before there is any evidence to confirm them, while we remain skeptical of experiments that seem to have no solid theoretical foundation. Anyone who delves deeply in the nature of science cannot help but come to the conclusion that we find the products of the human imagination more convincing than the things we observe. In the end, only experiment can determine whether a theory is true or false. But that is the end of the creative process in science, not the beginning.

FLOATING CONTINENTS

We're all familiar with the myth of the unheralded genius, the scientist whose theories are rejected by his colleagues, but who is finally vindicated, usually after he is dead. For the most part, it is exactly that: a myth. It is difficult to find many examples of this phenomenon in the history of science. Far more common is a case like that of Einstein. Many scientists doubted the special theory of relativity when it was first proposed. However, it was taken seriously enough to be subjected to experimental tests. And it was generally recognized that Einstein had made contributions in other areas of physics. For example, the same year that he propounded his special theory, he published a theoretical analysis that proved the existence of atoms. At the time, many physicists considered the existence of atoms to be a useful fiction that had no real basis in reality.

However, there exist some cases where a theory was initially rejected, and later proved to be true. The history of the phenomenon of hypnosis provides one example. When the English physician James Braid began to study hypnosis, and to publish his findings around the middle of the nineteenth century, his ideas met with violent opposition.

But this was largely because hypnosis was still associated with the theories of the eighteenth century Viennese physician Franz Mesmer. Mesmer called hypnosis "animal magnetism," and believed it to be an occult force. To make matters worse, Mesmer had been something of a charlatan. He would often treat his patients while wearing a long, flowing purple robe, while carrying a scepterlike iron rod in one hand. It is not surprising that scientists and medical men should have still doubted the reality of hypnosis in the time of Braid. In fact, they may even have been right. Some psychologists are again beginning to doubt the reality of hypnosis today.

A somewhat more clear cut example is provided by the career of Alfred Wegener, the German meteorologist who was the founder of the theory of plate tectonics or *continental drift*. Nowadays scientists believe that the earth's continents drift across the surface of the earth. When they collide with one another, mountain ranges are created. When they drift apart, they often leave telltale traces behind.

Anyone who has ever looked at a map of the continents of the southern hemisphere cannot help but have noticed that the coastlines of Africa and South America look as though they had once been fitted together. If this is so, then they must have drifted apart over long periods of geological time. It is only natural, then, to try and see if there exists other evidence that would indicate that Africa and South America were once connected.

Wegener realized that there was a great deal of evidence that would support a theory of continental drift. When he published his book *The Origins of Continents and Oceans* in 1915 it had long been known that there were striking similarities between fossils found on different continents. For example, fossils of *Mesosaurus*, a reptile that lived during the Paleozoic era (which ended about 245 million years ago) had been discovered in Brazil and in South Africa, and nowhere else.

Wegener also noted that similarities between living creatures existed. The lemur was found in both India and Africa, while the garden snail *Helix pomatia* was also found on continents that are now separated by oceans.

Biologists and geologists were well aware of such facts. But they adhered to the theory that these animals had migrated across land bridges that supposedly once connected distant continents. The absence of such land bridges today was explained by assuming that they had eventually subsided.

Wegener realized that this idea was not a very reasonable one. Not only was there no evidence that such land bridges had once existed, it also seemed impossible to explain their subsidence. Continental crust is made of granite, which is lighter than the basaltic rock that is found on the ocean floors. If the land bridges had been founded on granite too—and it was hard to see how they could have been composed of anything else—then one was forced to assume that a lighter material had sunk into a heavier one.

According to Wegener, the continents were giant rafts that floated on a heavier material. He found support for this idea in a discovery that had been made near the end of the nineteenth century. It was found that both Canada and Scandinavia were rising at the rate of about one centimeter per year. Apparently, the weight of the ice that had covered them during the last ice age had caused them to sink down into the basalt, and that process was now being reversed.

If continents could move in a vertical direction, Wegener reasoned, then there was no reason why they could not drift in a horizontal direction too. But Wegener did not limit himself to making this hypothesis. Instead, he looked for further evidence for continental drift. He soon found it. He discovered that there was geological evidence for the similarity of rock formations in the corresponding parts of Africa and South America. Furthermore, mountain ranges on opposing continents would link up with one another if the continents were brought together. The mountains in eastern Canada seemed to be a continuation of those in Norway and Scotland, and the Sierras of Argentina could be matched up with South Africa's Cape mountains. It was as though two pieces of a newspaper page that had been torn in half were fitted together.

You might think that, since Wegener had amassed so much evidence for his theory, it would have been readily accepted by other scientists. It wasn't. By the mid-1920s, Wegener's ideas had begun to arouse intense antagonism. Geologists and geophysicists, in particular, subjected his theory to violent attacks. There were no known forces, they said, that could cause continents to move about in such a manner. The whole idea was nonsense.

Some scientists took pains to explain Wegener's carefully accumulated evidence away. The rock formations on different continents, geologists said, were not as similar as he had claimed. Scientists also questioned his credentials. He was not a professional geologist, they pointed out. On the contrary, he was an amateur who took liberties with the globe. Disdain for Wegener's ideas became so strong, especially in the United States, that any geologist who expressed interest in them risked his professional reputation. Wegener died in 1930. By the 1940s, his theory was considered to have been entirely discredited. The rigid-earth theory had become geological dogma.

And yet, in the end, Wegener turned out to have been right. During the 1950s, new scientific instruments were devised that were capable of measuring magnetic fields ten million times weaker than that of the earth. When these instruments were used to measure the residual magnetism of old rock formations, new and surprising results were obtained. It was found that certain rocks contained a record of the earth's magnetic field at the time that the rocks were formed. When the magnetism of 200 million-year-old rocks found in the English countryside was measured, it was found that England had once been situated at a latitude of 30 degrees north. Its latitude is 65 degrees at the present time.

At first, geologists did not take this to be evidence that there had been any shift in the positions of terrestrial land masses. It was the earth's magnetic field that had changed, they concluded. But this theory of magnetic pole wandering soon encountered difficulties. When the magnetism of rocks from other continents was compared with that of the English rocks, different results were obtained. This was evidence that the relative positions of the continents had changed. The relative motion that they had exhibited was nothing other than Wegener's continental drift.

Not all scientists were convinced. But then, in 1962, the Princeton University geologist Harry H. Hess proposed a theory of sea floor spreading. Hot material from the earth's interior, he suggested, was constantly pushing its way to the surface through volcanic ridges on the ocean floor. As the lava cooled, it hardened into basaltic rock. But it did not remain motionless. The pressure of the material that continued to flow from the ridges pushed it outward in both directions. The ocean floors were made up of moving material. And obviously, if the ocean floors could move, so could the continents. Any continent that happened to be floating on one of these plates would experience continental drift.

The clincher came in 1963, when the British oceanographers Frederick J. Vine and Drummond H. Matthews carried out measurements of magnetism in the rock that made up the ocean floors, and found that sea floor spreading was indeed a real phenomenon. Other scientists quickly confirmed their results. And once Hess' theory of sea floor spreading had been confirmed, Wegener's theory became respectable. By the end of the 1960s it was almost universally accepted.

THE ROLE OF THEORY

I find the story of the initial rejection and final acceptance of Wegener's idea about continental drift to be interesting, not because it is a tale of a misunderstood and maligned scientist who was finally vindicated after his death, but because it so aptly illustrates the role that is played by scientific theories. Wegener's ideas were initially attacked because no one could understand what could possibly cause continents to move. They were rapidly accepted once Hess' theory of sea floor spreading proved to be correct.

The story is not a very typical one. When scientists reject an idea on the grounds that it cannot be adequately explained, they usually turn out to be right. They reject astrology because they see no way in which the planets could possibly influence our lives, or because there seems to be nothing that would explain why there should be a correlation between planetary movements and human character. The lack of evidence for the validity of astrology is telling, but it is not the only reason why astrology is considered to be psuedoscience. If a discovery were made that caused planetary influences to seem reasonable, scientists would immediately begin to look for confirming evidence. They are skeptical about the findings of parapsychologists because the existence of ESP supposedly depends on unknown paranormal forces. Here too, the lack of evidence plays a role, but it is not the most important factor.

Should science place so much emphasis on theory in preference to experiment? I suspect that those who would answer "no" have been misled about the nature of science. They have been taught the old Baconian idea that theories are generalizations of experience, that scientists work by induction, that they construct theoretical principles from repeated observations.

The nature of induction is an old philosophical problem that has never really been solved. If I observe a thousand crows and find that they are all black, I still cannot be sure that the thousand-and-first crow will not turn out to be white. But perhaps induction is not as vital to science as many have thought. If, instead of depending on inductive inferences, I study the genetics of the color of crows, I will likely find that I have very good reasons for thinking that the thousand-and-first bird will be black too. By doing so, I can find another confirmation of genetic theory, or at least subject it to the test of falsification. Simple observation generally gets us nowhere. It is the creative imagination that increases our understanding by finding connections between apparently unrelated phenomena, and forming logical, consistent theories to explain them. And if a theory turns out to be wrong, as many do, all is not lost. The struggle to create an imaginative, correct picture of reality frequently tells us where to go next, even when science has temporarily followed the wrong path.

NOTES

[1] These are described in detail in my book *Cosmic Questions*.

[2] I can't resist relating one of my favorite stories about Picasso here (which, like many such stories may or may not be apocryphal). It seems that a Parisian dealer had come into possession of a Picasso painting and doubted its authenticity. So he took it to Picasso himself. Picasso took one look, and said, "It's a fake!" Later, when the painting turned out to be genuine, Picasso was reproached by the dealer. "I often paint fakes," he replied.

[3] Interestingly, when Geller appeared on the Johnny Carson show, he was apparently unable to demonstrate any paranormal abilities. Some writers have suggested that perhaps he knew that Carson, who had once been a professional magician, would see through his tricks.

4 I say *apparently* because quantum mechanics is a theory that yields accurate quantitative predictions. We may sometimes have difficulty saying what it *really means*, but this does not alter its status as an extremely successful scientific theory.

5 This isn't true of all species, however. As the doctors at one hospital discovered to their dismay, there are some maggots that devour healthy flesh and leave the gangrenous tissue untouched.

CHAPTER 3

WHEN THE WORLD CHANGED

When Albert Einstein first became famous during the 1920s, members of the general public tended to think of him, not as a physicist, but as a mathematician. Einstein, they believed, was the mage who could discern the nature of the universe just by thinking abut it, and by working through the appropriate equations.

Popular images of famous people are not noted for their accuracy. But there was actually a great deal of truth in this one. In fact it is very close to ideas that Einstein expressed himself. For example, in his Herbert Spencer lecture, delivered at Oxford University in June of 1933, he stated that, "I am convinced that we can discover by means of purely mathematical constructions the concepts and the laws connecting them with each other, which furnish the key to the understanding of natural phenomena." He went on to say that, "In a certain sense, therefore, I hold it true that pure thought can grasp reality, as the ancients dreamed."

Einstein believed that there existed no inductive method that could lead to the fundamental concepts of physics. On the other hand if one could discover the simplest and most elegant possible mathematical description of a physical phenomenon, it was virtually guaranteed to be correct. To be sure, theories had to be tested. But the creative principle resided in an understanding of the mathematics and in theoretical vision.

This understanding did not come effortlessly. Einstein worked on his general theory of relativity for years until he found what he believed to be the correct mathematical description of the force of gravity. And he spent decades of his life trying to find a unified field theory, one that would describe both gravity and electromagnetic forces within the same framework. However, once he found an answer, he was generally certain that it had to be correct. He didn't find a unified field theory, of course. But in other areas of physics, his intuition was generally unerring.

I have already given an example of this: Einstein's feeling of certainty about the correctness of his general theory of relativity before any experimental tests were carried out. But I don't think that it would be unreasonable to emphasize the point by giving another.

Einstein's special theory of relativity of 1905 produced a number of predictions about the behavior of objects that traveled at high velocities. At the time, there was only one way to test the theory, by performing experiments with electrons. Since an electron is very light—its mass is about 1,830 times smaller than that of a proton—it can be accelerated to high velocities with relative ease. If an object is light, it will have a small resistance to motion. For example, it is a lot easier to throw a golf ball across the room than it is to push an automobile the same distance. Furthermore, an electron has an electric charge, which means that simple electrical apparatus can be used to accelerate it.

In 1906 the German physicist Walter Kaufmann published the results of a long series of experiments that he had performed with moving electrons. He found that his results agreed with some theories of electron motion and disagreed with others. In particular, they failed to substantiate the predictions of Einstein's special theory. There were small but significant differences between Kaufmann's results and Einstein's calculations.

But Einstein was not troubled. Commenting on the two theories that Kaufmann's experiments did seem to support, he said, "In my opinion both theories have a rather small probability [of being true] because their fundamental assumptions . . . are not explainable in terms of theoretical systems which embrace a greater complex of phenomena."

In other words, no matter what the experiments said, the competing theories could not be true because they did not fit into far-reaching, clear-cut theoretical patterns. Einstein had *seen* what physical reality had to be like. The other theorists hadn't.

In the end, of course, Einstein's insistence on the correctness of his theory turned out to be justified. More accurate experiments that were performed later gave precisely the results that were predicted by his theory. Today, the experimental support for his theory is overwhelming.

In a way, Einstein reminds one of Beethoven, who believed that when he created his music, he was seeing into the mind of God and of other romantic artists who had similar feelings. Einstein sometimes spoke of penetrating the secrets of the "Old One," and he often stated that he sought to discover how God had constructed the universe.

When he made such comments, he was not speaking of the God of Judaism and Christianity. He had lost his belief in a personal God while he was still an adolescent. Sometimes Einstein seemed to identify God with the order of the universe. On other occasions, he expressed views that were pantheistic in character. For example, when he responded to a query from a Rabbi Goldstein in New York in 1929 about his religious beliefs, Einstein replied that he believed in "Spinoza's God who reveals himself in the harmony of all that exists, not in a God who concerns himself with the fate and actions of men."

THE MYSTIC, THE CONSERVATIVE, AND THE PHILOSOPHER

Einstein was not a mystic in the religious or *spiritual* sense of the term. Yet there was something decidedly mystical about his outlook on the universe. He believed in a universal order that could be understood by an intuitive human mind. What is amazing about his outlook is that his intuitions were virtually always correct. If he was able to discern that the universe *had* to be a certain way, then that was more important than experiment. Of course, Einstein's theories were all confirmed by experiment in the end. If they had not been, it would be impossible to say that he had made significant contributions to physics.

Obviously, most theoretical physicists do not work the way that Einstein did. They couldn't; they don't possess the same kinds of minds. But Einstein did not create modern physics alone. There were many other scientists who made significant contributions that changed our way of looking at the universe.

One of them was Max Planck, the German physicist who founded quantum theory in 1900. Where Einstein was always willing to try out new ideas, Planck was very much a scientific conservative. He had been trained in nineteenth-century classical physics, and he considered it his duty to clear up some of the few (or so he thought) problems that remained.

One of these problems had to do with the emission of light and heat from matter. Nothing could be more obvious than the fact that temperature plays an important role in this phenomenon. If a piece of iron is heated, one can feel the heat that it radiates. If it is heated further, it will glow red hot, then white hot. But at the end of the nineteenth century, no one really knew how to describe this phenomenon mathematically. It was possible to write mathematical formulas that were derived from certain basic principles, but these formulas agreed with experiment only in certain temperature ranges. In other ranges, they gave results that were terribly wrong.

These formulas described an idealized object called a *blackbody*. It is true that there are no perfectly black objects in nature; every known substance reflects some light. However, it is possible to simulate the behavior of a blackbody in the laboratory. By Planck's time a great amount of experimental data about such simulated black-bodies had been obtained. Since the blackbody problem was so puzzling, Planck felt that he must expend a great deal of effort on it.

Planck considered the anomalies in the radiation laws to be a blemish in the structure of theoretical physics, one that must at all costs be removed. But Planck didn't attempt to make use of intuitive insights about nature the way that Einstein so often did. He worked in a much more practical manner. He began by looking for an equation that *did* work. Once he found it, he tried to imagine what physical phenomena would produce such a formula. He soon succeeded, and found that if this formula was correct, then it was necessary to assume that radiating bodies gave off energy in packets of a certain size, which he called quanta. One quantum of energy could be emitted, or two, or any whole number. But one could not have a situation in which one-and-a-half quanta or two and three-eighths were given off.

Planck didn't really relish having to make such an assumption. According to classical theory, there should have been no restrictions on the size of the bundles of energy that were emitted. The theory predicted that they could be very small, or very large, or any size in between. Planck was later to characterize the formation of his hypothesis as an "act of desperation," and he spent the next ten years of his life trying to find a way to avoid the seemingly bizarre result that he had obtained. When Einstein suggested in 1905 that light and other kinds of radiation actually traveled through space in the form of quanta (now called *photons*), he was horrified. Planck's quantum theory had suggested only that energy was emitted in this manner; he had assumed that, once it was emitted, it assumed the form of waves. After all, nothing else was consistent with classical physics. It had long been known that radiation was a wave phenomenon. And here was Einstein suggesting that radiation also had a particlelike character.

To the lay person, Planck's manner of doing physics may

seem very plodding, while Einstein's may be seen as awesome and mysterious. However, one shouldn't downgrade Planck's contributions to physics. He was one of the great theoretical physicists and it is he, not Einstein, who must be considered to be the founder of modern physics.

Planck and Einstein simply had different scientific styles. This was even reflected in their personal lives. Einstein is known for his long white hair, the sweatshirt that he liked to wear during his later years, and for the fact that he gave up wearing socks during that period of his life. Socks, he had discovered, get holes in them. Planck, on the other hand, had great respect for authority, and his manner was reserved and formal. He wore dark clothing and heavily starched shirts, and would leave home for his office at the university at exactly the same time every morning. A visitor in his household once observed that, just as the clock in the hall was sounding, Planck would emerge from his room and make his way to the front door.

Einstein is sometimes considered to have been something of a rebel. But this characterization is probably inaccurate. It is true that, as an adolescent, he rebelled against the regimentation in German schools. But in later life he was more likely to laugh at authority than to rebel against it. His outlook on life, and on social convention, has sometimes been characterized as bohemian. There is probably some truth in this point of view, although he wasn't bohemian in the way that many artists have been. Though he was somewhat poor when he was a university student, he never lived in real poverty, and he assiduously sought positions in major universities.

You might think that two people as different as Planck and Einstein would have had an antipathy toward one another. In reality, the opposite was the case. They respected one another as theoretical physicists. And, in fact, Planck was the earliest and most enthusiastic supporter of Einstein's theory of special relativity. This is not as surprising as it sounds. Many of the predictions of special relativity were indeed surprising. For example, Einstein spoke of bodies that simultaneously contracted and increased in mass as their velocities increased. But special relativity was really nothing more than an outgrowth of classical physics. It took some of the classical laws and expressed them in the context of a broader theoretical structure. If special relativity had not been discovered by Einstein, most likely someone else would have within a few years, or at most a decade.[1] In fact, when Einstein proposed the theory, the Dutch physicist Hendrik Lorentz and the French mathematician Henri Poincaré had already taken the first steps toward its discovery.

But of course Planck's admiration for Einstein's ideas was not boundless. When Einstein attempted to go beyond the boundaries of classical physics, Planck was likely to react differently. For example, when Planck proposed Einstein for membership in the Royal Prussian Academy of Science in 1912, he included a note of apology. Einstein's ideas about light quanta, Planck said, could not "really be held against him." Any physicist as creative as Einstein, he went on, was likely to occasionally miss the mark.

If one had to choose the three greatest figures in the development of modern physics, they would have to be Einstein, Planck, and the Danish physicist Niels Bohr. It was Bohr who created the first workable theory of the atom. In fact, when lay people picture an atom, they generally think of it the way that Bohr did: as an object composed of electrons that orbit around a nucleus. Bohr's theory has since been superseded by those of quantum mechanics. We now know that it is more accurate to think of electrons as wave patterns centered around the nucleus. Nevertheless, Bohr's theory was accurate enough that it can still be used under certain circumstances.

Bohr did not invent the idea that atoms are composed of nuclei that are surrounded by electrons. When he proposed his atomic theory in 1913, this was already known. But Bohr was the first to gain an understanding of how atoms actually worked. In particular, his theory explained Planck's results. According to Bohr, electrons could spontaneously jump from one orbit to another. When they did, they gave up some of their energy in the form of radiation. Bohr's theory made it possible to calculate the energy difference between orbits, and these energy differences corresponded to Planck's quanta.

According to Bohr, only certain specific orbits were possible. This meant that an electron could have energy A or energy B but it could not have any energy in between. Such electron orbits were said to be *quantized*. Bohr did not explain why the orbits should be quantized, or how an electron could make a spontaneous quantum jump from one to another. But his theory did conform to experimental data, at least from data obtained from the study of the simpler atoms. Bohr later used his theory to explain the behavior of the chemical elements, suggesting that electrons within a complex atom were arranged in concentric shells. It was the behavior of the electrons in the outermost shell that gave the elements their particular properties.

Bohr's theory was later superseded by the theory of quantum mechanics, which was developed independently by the German physicist Werner Heisenberg and the Austrian physicist Erwin Schrödinger in the years 1925-26. However, quantum mechanics retained many of the ideas of the *old quantum theory* that was developed by Bohr and his colleagues. For example, in quantum mechanics, only certain energy states are possible, and there are still quantum jumps between them. Bohr's theory was not so much discarded as improved upon, and much of the early work on quantum mechanics was done at Bohr's Institute for Theoretical Physics in Copenhagen.

Today, much is written about the bizarre, supposedly paradoxical character of quantum mechanics. So perhaps I should emphasize the fact that the theory itself has never been called into question. The arguments that one hears do not question the validity of quantum mechanics as a scientific theory, they deal with the philosophical problem of interpreting the picture that quantum mechanics gives us of the subatomic world. The physicists who use quantum mechanics in their work do not have to worry about its meaning. The theory works, and it works very well. But if we want to know precisely what quantum mechanics tells us about the nature of reality, we encounter problems that have never been solved, or which are at least open to different interpretations.

Bohr was the first to think about the philosophical problem of the interpretation of the theory, and he discussed the problems that arose with other scientists who visited his institute, which became a kind of Mecca for theoretical physicists. The interpretation of quantum mechanics that was developed under Bohr's guidance is called the *Copenhagen interpretation*, and it is still the most widely accepted today.

Basically, the problem was this: Quantum mechanics described the behavior of subatomic particles in terms of probabilities. For example, if an electron is shot at a fluorescent screen, one can observe a pinpoint of light when it arrives. This is the principle on which television is based. A very large number of electrons, each of which produce a small quantity of light, can be used to create a television picture. Now quantum mechanics only allows one to predict the probability that the electron will strike the screen at one spot or another. But when the collision actually takes place, we find that it has arrived at a very specific place. Somehow the probability has been transformed into a certainty. When a television image is created, this is no problem. The number of electrons hitting the screen is so large that the probabilities would average out anyway. But in the case of a single particle, it is not so easy to tell what is going on.

The phenomenon of radioactive decay is another example. For example, some atomic nuclei will emit alpha particles (charged particles consisting of two protons and two neutrons). According to quantum mechanics, there is no way to predict when the decay of any individual nucleus will happen. In reality a nucleus will decay at some very specific point in time. Again, if there are large numbers of nuclei, there is no problem. We can say, for example, that half of them will decay in the next fifteen minutes, or in the next four hours, or in the next billion years. This is where the term *half-life* comes from.

There was also another, related problem. By the time that quantum mechanics was developed it was known that particles sometimes behaved as though they were particles, and sometimes as waves. Light and other forms of radiation had the same characteristic. Einstein had been right when he had suggested that light could travel through space in the form of quanta (or photons, as we would say now). But a particle never exhibited both wave and particle characteristics at the same time. In one experiment an electron could appear as a wave, in another as a particle. It appeared that the experimenter had a choice as to which property he wanted to observe. Whichever one he decided upon, the electron would willingly comply.

The interpretation that was developed by Bohr and his colleagues at the Copenhagen Institute was this: a subatomic particle had no objective properties until it was observed. It was the act of observation that forced it to make one choice or another. I think that perhaps I can make this point a little clearer by giving yet another example. According to Heisenberg's famous uncertainty principle, it is impossible to determine the position and the momentum of an electron (or of any other subatomic particle) at the same time. The more accurately one knows the momentum (or velocity, since momentum is just mass times velocity; the only reason that physicists speak of momentum is that it fits into their mathematical formulas in a more convenient manner), the less one can tell about the particle's position. This has nothing to do with the accuracy of one's measuring instruments. It is a fundamental fact of nature.

According to Bohr's Copenhagen interpretation, an electron did not *have* a specific position or a specific velocity until a measurement was made. Position and momentum were not objectively real properties until one or the other was measured.

All this sounds very bizarre, but the other choices seem no less paradoxical. For example, the California Institute of Technology physicist Richard Feynman developed a *sum over histories* interpretation. According to Feynman, an electron that travels from point A to point B follows *all* possible paths between the two points. But all possible paths are not equal; the probability of some of them cancel one another out. Feynman's idea and Bohr's can be used to interpret the same phenomena. The quantitative predictions produced by the theory are the same in either case. After all, we are speaking about interpretations. But they give somewhat different pictures of reality. There is also a *many worlds* interpretation of quantum mechanics, according to which a new alternate universe is created whenever a particle has to make one choice or another. This sounds even crazier than Bohr's and Feynman's interpretations, but it is consistent with the observed facts, and again it can be used to explain the same phenomena. Presumably one could never observe any of these alternate universes. But then one can't catch an electron in the act of deciding whether it should have a well-defined position or a well-defined momentum either.

Bohr's ideas were accepted by many physicists, but not by Einstein, who would have nothing to do with them. In his mind, Bohr's conception of subatomic reality lacked the inner harmony that he demanded of a scientific theory. In particular, he argued that, if quantum mechanics seemed to depend upon probabilities, this could only mean that the theory was not *complete*. That is, there had to be some deeper, as yet undiscovered theory, in which the probabilities would disappear. "God does not play dice," he would say again and again. On one occasion, an exasperated Bohr chided Einstein in reply, saying that Einstein had no right to dictate what God should do.

The argument continued for more than a decade. Einstein would invent imaginary *thought experiments* that supposedly showed that quantum mechanics could not be a complete theory. Bohr would respond by showing flaws in Einstein's reasoning. But Einstein never gave up. He continued to oppose the Copenhagen interpretation of quantum mechanics until the end of his life.

Today, most physicists believe that Bohr was right and that Einstein was wrong. Theoretical work and experimental results are shown that if one wants to give up the idea that the subatomic world is not inherently probabilistic,[2] it is necessary to accept even more unpalatable ideas. In particular, it has been shown that, if quantum mechanics is not a complete theory, then it should be possible to send signals that travel faster than the speed of light. Now, if this were possible, then, according to Einstein's special theory of relativity, it should be possible also to send signals from the future into the past.[3] It is not possible to prove that this cannot happen, but it would upset the notions of causality on which all physical science is based. After all, if it is possible to send signals to the past, the past could be changed.

The story of the creation of modern physics is a tale of great achievements that transformed our understanding of the world around us. But it is also a story of conflicting scientific styles. On one hand, there was the conservative Planck, who enthusiastically embraced Einstein's relativity theory, which fit in so well with classical physics, but who would have repudiated his own quantum theory if he had been able to find a way to do it. There was the philosophical Bohr, who made important contributions to atomic theory, but who expended at least as much effort on discussions with his colleagues about the meaning of quantum mechanics. And then there was Einstein the mystic, who was sometimes wrong, but who awed and mystified everybody. Obviously style played an important role in their scientific achievements. One could say that, stylistically, they were as different as Bach, Mozart, and Stravinsky.

ALBERT EINSTEIN AND JOE MONTANA

Although the parallels between scientific and artistic creativity are interesting, I think that it would be a mistake to try to make too much of them. There are at least as many differences as there are similarities. In any case, it is no longer fashionable to engage in armchair philosophizing about such matters. It has become a problem in cognitive psychology. It is true that no one can yet say precisely what creativity *is*. But at least we can approach such questions scientifically nowadays. I'll say no more abut this particular matter, however. Going into matters pertaining to contemporary psychology would lead us too far astray.

Nevertheless there do seem to be certain eerie connections. For example, musical talent and a talent for mathematics often seem to go together. Furthermore, music, mathematics, and chess are the only fields in which there are child prodigies. There must be something about the musical mind that is akin to the mind of a great mathematician. But it is not so easy to say exactly what this quality might be. It will not do to say that music is the most mathematical of the arts. Mozart would go for a walk and hear melodies in his head. Mathematicians have never reported hearing melodies in their heads as they proved theorems, not even mathematical ones.

As I think I have demonstrated, there are different scientific styles, just as there are styles in the arts. The authorship of a painting by Monet or a Van Gogh is unmistakable (unless, of course, it is a forgery). Certain stylistic qualities can often be seen in a scientific paper by Einstein. He typically made few references to the previous scientific literature, while presenting arguments that were pure and unadorned. But the existence of different styles may not have any significant implications beyond the fact that different human beings think and work differently. The scientific work of Einstein and that of Bohr were stylistically different. But then different plumbers have different styles too.

At one time it was fashionable to see parallels between the birth of the modernist movement in literature and that of the twentieth-century revolution in physics. At first glance, this does not seem like an unreasonable idea. After all, they began at abut the same time. But there the resemblances cease. The revolution in physics happened because new discoveries had been made, and they had somehow to be explained. X rays were discovered in 1895, radioactivity shortly thereafter. In 1900 Planck found that blackbody radiation could only be explained if it was assumed that radiation was emitted in the form of quanta. In the meantime, ongoing series of experiments failed to detect the ether, the hypothetical medium that was thought to transmit both gravitational forces and electromagnetic waves. The physicists of the day were not able to understand how waves could be propagated if they lacked something to *wave in* and they were uncomfortable with the idea of gravity as action at a distance (even Newton had expressed discomfort about the idea). They attempted to solve these problems by assuming that there existed an elastic, incomprehensible fluid that filled all space. The only problem was that, as far as anyone could tell, the ether just wasn't there. But it took an Einstein to suggest that the idea of the ether was *superfluous*. And once he realized that it was, he was well on the way to developing his special theory of relativity.

One of the authors who suggested that there were parallels between modernism in the arts and modernism in physics was the British novelist Lawrence Durrell. He discussed the matter at length in his book, *A Key to Modern British Poetry* (University of Oklahoma Press, 1952). However, Durrell succeeded only in demonstrating that he hadn't the slightest idea of what modern physics was all about. Perhaps one shouldn't criticize him too harshly for this; the enthusiasm of an amateur can be a wonderful thing even when it leads to errors in understanding. In any case, Durrell was really only elaborating on a suggestion, made by the English author and painter Wyndham Lewis that the artist receives "blindly...all kinds of notions and formulae" from fields outside his own. Presumably this would include scientific fields. This is an appealing notion. The only problem with it, when applied to scientific ideas, is the fact that most artists don't understand science very well. For example, it is hard to see how they could be influenced by relativity when, more often than not, they share the popular misconception that relativity has something to do with the doctrine of relativism (it doesn't; what Einstein's theory really says is that the laws of physics must be the same for any observer). Conversely, it is not very likely that Einstein was influenced by the development of cubism.

Thus the idea put forward by Lewis and Durrell (and by the Austrian art historian Sigfried Giedon, among others) seems to be as questionable as the notion that there are parallels between quantum mechanics and eastern mysticism. If anything, it is easier to find parallels between theoretical physics and the game of football. It has been noted that the career of a theoretical physicist bears a chronological resemblance to that of a football quarterback. Physicists generally make their most important contributions when they are quite young. Einstein was twenty-six when he published his papers on the special theory of relativity. Newton was about the same age when he discovered his law of gravitation. And today, theoretical scientists often receive the Nobel prize for work done in their doctoral dissertations.

As a theoretical physicist ages, he generally exhibits a marked falling off in creativity. Einstein, for example, made all of his important contributions before the age of forty. It is true that physicists generally go on working until they retire (unless they become administrators). But they generally do little more than elaborate upon previous work.

If one were to chart Einstein's creativity (this could easily be done simply by citing the number of important papers written at different periods of time), the chart would look very much like one that depicted the statistics of Joe Montana.

And what are the implications of all this? There are probably none of any significance. A football player is often considered *old* if he is over thirty. The same is true of a chess grandmaster or a theoretical physicist. This simply demonstrates that a young mind or a young body can sometimes be used to achieve things that become more difficult as one grows older.

It also suggests that, when human beings want to, they are probably capable of seeing parallels between any two things, however dissimilar they may be.

NOTES

[1] This is not true of Einstein's general theory of relativity, however. If there had never been an Einstein, the theory probably would not have been found for decades.

[2] Probability enters into all the various interpretations in one way or another.

[3] The paradoxes associated with sending signals into the past are discussed in detail in my book *Achilles in the Quantum Universe* (Holt, 1997).

CHAPTER 4
PLATONISTS AND KANTIANS

We have all had the experience of seeing two dogs, or two onions, or of watching a baseball game in which a particular player got two hits. But none of us has ever seen the number 2. Here, I am not referring to the Arabic numeral 2, which we frequently see printed on paper, but to the abstract idea that 2 represents. This is clearly not the same as the printed numeral, which can also be written as *II* in Roman numerals, or as *10* in the binary notation that is used by computers. This suggests the question: "Is the number 2 something real, or is it an invention of the human mind?"

Not all mathematicians would give the same answer. Some of them, who are often referred to as *Platonists*, maintain that numbers, and all other mathematical objects as well, are real objects, and that the relationships between them are discovered from human beings. This view was expressed very clearly by the British mathematician G.H. Hardy. In his book, *A Mathematician's Apology* (Cambridge University Press, 1941), Hardy said:

> I will state my position dogmatically in order to avoid minor misapprehensions. I believe that mathematical reality lies outside us, that our function is to discover or observe it, and that the theorems which we prove, and which we describe grandiloquently as our "creations," are simply notes of our observations.

To some extent, calling mathematicians who would agree with Hardy *Platonists* is a little misleading. It is true that Plato also believed that mathematical objects were real things. But he also believed that all abstract ideas, such as *beauty, justice,* and *truth* represented something real. Furthermore, he extended this idea to many other more mundane concepts. He thought, for example, that the concept *tree* possessed the same kind of reality, and that the trees that were seen in the everyday world were only imperfect copies of it. Few people today subscribe to Plato's philosophy, and the mathematicians we call *Platonists* usually don't either when something other than a mathematical concept is being considered.

On the other hand, there are numerous mathematicians, whom we might call *Kantians*, who subscribe to the idea that mathematics is wholly a creation of the human mind. According to their view, mathematical ideas are not discovered, they are created by human beings. The term *Kantian*, naturally, is no more accurate than *Platonist*. The eighteenth-century German philosopher Immanuel Kant believed that the world was basically unknowable, and that such concepts as space and time existed only within the human mind. It was these innate concepts that allowed us to interpret the phenomena that we perceived in the world around us, he said. Furthermore, we could never really know the reality that lay behind these phenomena. The role that Kant assigned to the human mind gives some justification for calling this class of mathematicians *Kantian*, and the term has been used to describe them, although not so often as *Platonist*. But naturally few of them would subscribe to Kant's philosophy in toto. They generally believe only that mathematics—not the entire phenomenal world—is a human creation.

PLATO AMONG THE PHYSICISTS

You probably won't be very surprised if I say that few physicists have expressed Kantian views about their subject. After all, physics studies real natural phenomena. Such things as gravity, the heat and light that come to us from the sun, and the pockets of turbulent air that often affect commercial aircraft are things that we see and feel. It would be absurd to regard them as mental objects.

Something similar can be said of the physical entities that we can't see. For example, a magnetic field is more than an abstract idea. It is something whose presence can be detected by anyone who has a coil of wire and some kind of instrument that will detect small electric currents. If the coil of wire is placed between two poles of a magnet, an electrical current will be set up. This current can then be measured without any difficulty. It is even possible to observe subatomic particles with the naked eye, since they will produce tiny flashes on a fluorescent screen when they strike it. In such a case, it is very difficult to deny that *something* must have hit the screen. We can see photons without any equipment. It is thought that as few as one or two photons are sufficient to elicit a response in a dark-adapted eye.

Nevertheless, there have been some scientists who have had a Kantian outlook. At the end of the nineteenth century, for example, there were a few physicists who refused to accept the existence of atoms. They knew as well as anyone else that it was necessary to assume that atoms and molecules existed in order to explain the facts of chemistry. They knew also that the properties of a gas could be explained, that it was made up of molecules that were in a state of rapid, random motion. Nevertheless, they maintained that atoms (and hence molecules) were nothing more than a useful fiction. Physicists should not assume the existence of entities that could not be seen or otherwise detected, they said.

But then, in 1905, Einstein published a paper, which, once and for all, established the existence of molecules and presumably of atoms. He performed a theoretical analysis of the Brownian movement, a phenomenon that had been discovered by the Scottish botanist Robert Brown in 1827. When Brown studied pollen grains that were suspended in water with a microscope, he noted that the individual grains moved about in an irregular manner.

At first he thought that the pollen grains must move because they were living matter. Life, he concluded, must somehow be contained within the grains. But when he suspended particles of dye, which could not be alive, he observed the same phenomenon.

Now a grain of pollen, or of dye, or any other material visible under the microscope, is far too large to be affected by collisions with individual molecules. So the nature of the Brownian movement remained a mystery, even after scientists had become convinced of the molecular makeup of matter. It remained a mystery, that is, until Einstein showed that collisions with large numbers of molecules would have exactly the desired effect. His theoretical calculations showed, not only that the suspended particles would move, but also that they would move in a manner that was consistent with experimental data.

Today, no reputable scientist doubts the existence of atoms, or of the electrons, protons, and neutrons that are their components. Individual atoms can be seen with an instrument called the tunneling scanning microscope (a type of electron microscope), and it is possible to perform experiments in which individual particles are isolated and studied. For example, Nobel laureate Hans Dehmelt, a physicist at the University of Washington, has developed apparatus that can trap and isolate a single electron for periods of months, and physicists who do experiments concerning quantum mechanics will often observe the path or paths followed by a single neutron.

The idea that atoms are only useful fictions is discredited. It has been shown that they are not objects that exist only in scientists' minds (and in their equations). They have a real existence in the real world. However, questions about the reality of objects described by theoretical physicists were raised again when California University of Technology physicist Murray Gell-Mann proposed in 1964 that protons, neutrons, and many of the other particles that physicists had discovered were made up of even smaller particles called quarks. Some physicists responded by suggesting that quarks were fictional. These subatomic particles might behave *as though* they had quark components. But one shouldn't necessarily conclude that these tiny particles were real.

The skeptics appealed to the lack of experimental evidence for the existence of quarks. After Gell-Mann proposed his theory, searches for quarks were performed in numerous laboratories around the world. Without exception, the results were negative. Free quarks were not found in sea water, or in the cosmic rays that bombarded Earth from space, or anywhere else. But before long, theoretical physicists who thought that the quark was a real particle proposed an explanation for this. Quarks, they said, were bound together by a force that grew stronger as the particles moved farther apart. Thus any quarks that attempted to escape its bounds within a subatomic particle would be quickly pulled back. To be sure, this force was unlike any that physicists had previously encountered. Gravity and electromagnetic forces, for example, become weaker with increasing distance, not stronger. However, there were good theoretical reasons for thinking that this theoretical description of quark forces was an accurate one.

What exactly is the difference between a fictional particle and one that is real but which can never be observed? If there is any difference, it is a subtle one. To some physicists, saying that quarks were real was like saying that genies really existed, but that they were all sealed in bottles that were hidden in the depths of the ocean. To be sure, they said, the quark theory explained important subatomic phenomena. It explained what the difference between a proton and a neutron was, for example. Both particles have approximately the same mass (the neutron is just slightly heavier), but the proton has a positive electric charge, while the neutron—as the name implies—is electrically neutral. According to Gell-Mann's theory, each particle was composed of three quarks with fractional electric charges. In the proton, the charges added up to give +1; in the neutron they canceled out to give 0.

As it turned out, the doubts about the reality of the quark were not to last long. In 1968, an experiment was performed at the Stanford Linear Accelerator Center (SLAC) in which protons were bombarded with high-energy electrons. It was discovered that pointlike charges existed within the protons. Protons, it appeared, were made up of component particles. The existence of quarks was something that had to be taken seriously.

THE UNREASONABLE EFFECTIVENESS OF MATHEMATICS

One might expect that the controversy about the nature of mathematics might spill over into physics. After all, mathematics is the language of physics. But this has not been the case. Physicists generally don't pay much attention to questions about what mathematics is. If it works, that is enough for them. Physicists are also known for using mathematical methods that are not very rigorous. The mathematicians are sometimes horrified by what they do. But the physicists don't much care as long as the correct answer is obtained.

I think the reason for this is that, to a typical physicist, mathematical quantities are not abstractions. When he speaks of the number two, he may have two electrons in mind, or two different energy states of an atom. It is true that physicists sometimes deal with very abstract quantities, the *curved* space of Einstein, for example. But if the equations that describe such quantities can be manipulated in such a way that they yield predictions that can be tested by experiment, that is all they ask.

Physicists and mathematicians use mathematics so differently that some scientists have expressed surprise that it should be such an effective tool for the natural science. For example, the Hungarian-American physicist Eugene Wigner wrote of "the unreasonable effectiveness of mathematics." In a 1959 essay on the subject, he concluded that "The miracle of the appropriateness of mathematics for the formulation of the laws of physics is a wonderful gift which we neither understand nor deserve."

I would guess that most physicists do not know what Platonism and Kantianism in mathematics are. Those that do rarely trouble to apply these ideas to physics. Their approach is more pragmatic: if it works, use it. They may not know why a particular kind of mathematical concept seems to work, but if it does, that is all that seems to matter.

TACHYONS AND OTHER BEASTS

By now, you're probably wondering why I brought up the subject of Platonist and Kantian outlooks in the first place. They seem to have little or no relevance to physics. And, as we have seen, the view that atoms or quarks were only useful fictions was discredited. In fact, the story would end there if not for the fact that, during the second half of the twentieth century, theoretical physics probed so deeply into the structure of matter and into the nature of the universe that such questions arose again, this time with a vengeance.

During the mid-1960s physicists Gerald Feinberg and George Sudarshan showed independently that Einstein's special theory of relativity did not really rule out the possibility that particles might exist that traveled faster than the speed of light. According to Einstein's theory, no object that is traveling slower than light can ever reach light velocity. However, Feinberg and Sudarshan pointed out, kinds of particles might exist whose velocity always exceeded this limit. If they existed, they would encounter the "light barrier" from the other side. They could never travel at lower-than-light speeds. These hypothetical particles were named *tachyons*.

If tachyons existed, they would have to have a number of unusual properties. For example, unlike ordinary particles their energy would decrease—not increase—as their speed increased. In fact, their energy would become zero when they traveled at infinite velocity. In other words, an expenditure of energy would be required to slow a tachyon down. This is the opposite of what happens in the case of ordinary objects. For example, particle accelerators expend energy in order to get electrons, protons, and other particles moving at velocities close to that of light.

After Feinberg and Sudarshan made their suggestion, a number of experimental searches for tachyons were made. In every case, the results were negative. If tachyons really existed, either they did not interact with ordinary matter, or they interacted with it so weakly that it was impossible to detect their presence. Tachyons, it seemed, were nothing more than a theoretical possibility.

Feinberg no longer believes in tachyons. He points to the lack of experimental evidence to justify his view. The existence of tachyons cannot be ruled out completely. But anyone who wants to assume that they are real is faced with an interesting philosophical problem. Suppose that tachyons do exist, and that we can never detect them. In such a case, it is not so easy to say what the term *existence* means. It is generally applied only to objects in our own universe. But what if there were also a faster-than-light universe with which we could never interact? If we could never detect its presence, would we be justified in calling it *real?*

The example of tachyons does show, I think, that even in physics it is possible to speak of entities that may be nothing more than creations of the human mind. Tachyons may have no real existence, either in our universe or in another (whatever that means). Nevertheless it is possible to deduce their properties and to mathematically describe their behavior. Statements can be made about a tachyon's mass, about its momentum (which never becomes zero, no matter how fast it may travel), and about its energy. We may not know what these statements really mean, but they are certainly mathematically valid.

INFINITE WORLDS

In 1600 the Italian philosopher Giordano Bruno was burned at the stake for his various heresies. We can't be entirely sure precisely what the heresies were because scholars have never found a list of the charges against Bruno. But it is reasonable to assume that one of them was his doctrine that the universe contained an infinite number of inhabited worlds.

Naturally Bruno's condemnation by the Inquisition aroused great interest in his ideas. During the century that followed, the idea of an infinite universe became a commonplace of western thought. One suspects that this might not have happened if Bruno had not been burned. Bruno was a philosopher, not a scientist. But his persecution by Roman Catholic authorities publicized his ideas just as it publicized Galileo's.

Contemporary scientists are not sure whether the universe is infinite or finite. According to Einstein's general theory of relativity, it could be either. But this fact does not deter them from discussing the possibility of the existence of other universes, perhaps an infinite number of them. Most of us think of the big bang as something that happened once. In reality, it may be, as some scientists point out, something that has happened many times.

Some of the speculation about other universes is based upon the idea of wormholes. Wormholes are hypothetical gateways in space that would connect distant parts of the universe with one another. If they exist, they could not be used for interstellar travel like the wormhole in the television series *Star Trek Deep Space 9*. On the contrary, they would be microscopic objects with dimensions many orders of magnitude smaller than an atomic nucleus. Though a space vehicle obviously could not pass through them, many subatomic particles presumably could. In fact, according to one hypothesis, the mass of the electron can be attributed to the fact that electrons are constantly traveling through wormholes from one universe to another.

For that matter, there is no reason why our universe could not constantly be producing tiny *buds*, little bubbles of spacetime that are connected to our universe by microscopic wormholes. If it did, these *baby universes* (Stephen Hawking's term) could break off and grow into full-fledged universes after experiencing big bangs of their own.

BLACK HOLES AND BABY UNIVERSES

Stephen Hawking has suggested that the formation of black holes leads to the creation of other universes. His hypothesis makes use of the fact that no one really knows what happens after a dying, massive star undergoes catastrophic collapse. If the remnants of the star are massive enough, a black hole will form. As the matter that once made up the star falls inward, a point will soon be reached where gravity becomes so intense that nothing, not even light, can escape its bounds. The stellar remnant will become completely black because light can neither escape from nor be reflected by it.

But the gravitational collapse will not halt at this point. According to the general theory of relativity, it will continue until all of the matter within the black hole becomes compressed into a single mathematical point. If pressure develops, this will not halt the expansion. According to general relativity, the existence of pressure makes gravity even stronger.

The idea of compressing large quantities of matter within a single point so that a state of infinite density is reached is one that we need not take very seriously. When the dimensions of the shrinking ball of matter became very small, quantum effects would begin to become important. No one knows what these effects would be because a quantum theory of gravity would be required to explain the behavior of matter under such circumstances. But no quantum theory of gravity has ever been discovered. General relativity and quantum mechanics seem to be incompatible.

When one does not know what is happening, and has no good way of finding out, it is possible to make guesses. This is precisely what Hawking has done. He has suggested that the matter in the center of a black hole will travel through a wormhole to a newly formed baby universe. This is quite a daring idea. There is no way of showing that this actually happens. But then it is not possible to prove that the hypothesis is wrong either. Naturally, it depends upon certain assumptions. And there is no way of knowing whether or not these assumptions are correct.

Hawking's idea is only one of a number of different treatments of the many-universe idea. Many of them depend upon certain phenomena predicted by quantum mechanics. It has long been known that subatomic particles can be created out of pure energy, the energy in a gamma ray, for example. When this happens, the energy disappears and a particle-antiparticle pair appears in its place. For example, the two new particles might be an electron and a positron. The positron is the antiparticle of the electron. It and the electron have the same mass, but the positron has a positive electric charge, while that of the electron is negative. Not only can electrons and positrons be created out of pure energy, they also undergo mutual annihilation when they encounter one another, transforming themselves into a burst of energy again.

Now quantum mechanics is a theory that describes sub-atomic reality in terms of uncertainties. According to Heisenberg's uncertainty principle, the position and momentum (or velocity, if you prefer, since momentum = mass × velocity) of a particle cannot be determined at the same time. Now it so happens that the uncertainty principle can be applied to other pairs of quantities. Two such quantities are energy and time. If we know exactly how much energy an atom has, for example, we are able to say nothing about the length of time it will remain in that energy state.

It turns out that the energy-time relation has important physical consequences. The uncertainties in energy that exist during very short time periods can give rise to the creation of particle-antiparticle pairs. But, unlike real particles, these virtual particles cannot exist for very long. If a virtual electron-positron pair is created, for example, the two particles will annihilate one another within a tiny fraction of a billionth of a second.

Obviously, there is no way that the presence of virtual particles can be directly observed. You might wonder, therefore, if they might not be a useful fiction. But as it turns out, they are not. The creation of virtual particles has certain experimental consequences. Experimental tests of the virtual particle hypothesis have confirmed theoretical predictions to an accuracy of better than one part in 10 billion. Quantum fluctuations—the creation of such pairs of particles out of nothing—are apparently real.

This has led a number of physicists to speculate about the question of whether or not our universe may not have had its origin in a quantum fluctuation of some kind. In fact, there are a number of different variations on the idea. Although physicists have no theory of quantum gravity and thus do not really know what is going on in the realm of the very small, some have suggested that space and time themselves might be subject to quantum fluctuations. If they are, then there is no reason why a tiny, submicroscopic bubble of spacetime could not spontaneously appear. Some such bubbles might be expanding, others contracting. There is no reason why an expanding bubble could not grow into a full-fledged universe.

This idea was first suggested by the American physicist Edward Tryon in 1973. Tryon's proposal wasn't a fully worked-out theory. But it apparently sounded like a good idea, for other physicists soon began to elaborate upon it. In 1978, four Belgian physicists suggested that the universe may have begun with the creation of a single particle-antiparticle pair. And in 1981, physicists Heinz Pagels and David Atkatz of Rockefeller University proposed the idea that our universe might have begun, not with the creation of particles, but with a sudden change in the dimensionality of space. According to this theory the universe originally contained no matter and had a large number of spatial dimensions. The big bang might have taken place, Pagels and Atkatz suggested, when the universe *crystallized* into its present form. Of course this doesn't explain where the previously existing multidimensional universe came from. But this is not a serious impediment to the theory. It might always have existed, or it might also have been created in a quantum fluctuation of some sort.

Yet another hypothesis has been suggested by Tufts University physicist Alexander Vilenkin. According to Vilenkin, the universe may have emerged out of a kind of *quantum fuzz* that had no definite dimensionality. According to this theory, the very concepts of space and time have meaning only after the universe came into existence. One doesn't have to worry what happened before the big bang. There was no *before*. The idea that space and time began with the big bang, incidentally, is not unique to Vilenkin's theory. It is an assumption shared by many physicists and cosmologists. What was new about Vilenkin's hypothesis was his idea about the manner in which the universe came into existence.

Finally, physicist Andrei Linde of Stanford University has proposed a theory in which the problem of ultimate origins is avoided entirely. According to his *chaotic inflationary universe* hypothesis, new universes are being created all the time through a budding process. Unlike Hawking, Linde makes no appeal to black holes. In his theory the budding is a spontaneous process. Here, the term *inflationary* is a reference to the idea that, shortly after the big bang, the universe underwent a short period of very rapid, *inflationary* expansion. The original inflationary universe theory, which was developed by the American physicist Alan Guth, said nothing about origins. Linde's theory elaborates on some of his ideas.

According to Linde's theory, our universe began as a tiny bud that broke off from some previous universe. After it did, it experienced an inflationary expansion, and soon evolved into a full-fledged universe in its own right. Furthermore, Linde says, our universe may be giving birth to new universes right now. Since these baby universes are initially connected to our universe by submicroscopic wormholes that we cannot see, there is no way to observe this process.

According to Linde's theory the number of possible universes that come into existence might be limitless. Many of them would not bear any great resemblance to our universe. In some of them, inflationary expansions might never get started. In others, the period of inflation might never stop. But of course so many universes would be produced that there would likely be a great many like ours. And of course at least some of these might be inhabited.

UNIVERSES OF THE MIND

If there is one thing that all these hypotheses have in common, it is the fact that it seems impossible to test them. We can't travel back in time to a point shortly after the beginning of the universe to see what was really going on. Nor can we travel into black holes to see what happens as the matter within the hole undergoes a catastrophic collapse. Any space vehicle that ventured inside would be torn apart by gravitational forces. If it and its occupants somehow managed to survive, they still would not be able to send signals to the outside universe. The intense gravity would prevent that. It would not only prevent light from escaping, it would have the same effect on any kind of electromagnetic radiation, such as radio waves.

The various theories about the origin of the universe have a certain amount of plausibility, at least to someone who understands quantum mechanics. But there is no way to tell which, if any of them, is likely to be correct. Again, we can't travel back to the origin of the universes to see what was happening, and we can't see the wormholes that might connect our universe to baby universes before they break off and begin to grow into full-scale universes of their own. And of course other universes are things that we cannot observe, almost by definition. We simply could not communicate with a region of spacetime that had been separated from ours. The definition of our universe as *all that exists* may no longer be entirely accurate. But we can certainly say that our universe is all that we can see.

Theoretical physics and theoretical cosmology have gone so far that they no longer have any connection with observation and experiment. It would not be unfair to call the objects in the various scenarios that I have discussed *universes of the mind.* And cosmology is not the only field in which something like this has happened. In the last decade or so, there has been a great deal of theoretical speculation about superstrings, tiny ten-dimensional (i.e., nine dimensions of space and one of time) objects that might give rise to all of the known subatomic particles. The problem with superstrings is not so much their dimensionality (the fact that we see only four of the ten dimensions can be explained), but that they have dimensions many orders of magnitude smaller than that of an atomic nucleus. It is fair to assume that we will never be able to see them. Even a particle accelerator the size of our galaxy would not be able to probe the nature of matter at that level. Quarks can be *seen* in the sense that their presence affects the paths of electrons that are used to probe the interior of protons. And there have been numerous other experiments that have confirmed that it was quarks that the electrons in the SLAC experiment really *saw*. But we cannot build an accelerator large and powerful enough to see superstrings. Of course, in the end, theoretical physicists may decide that ten-dimensional superstrings do not exist after all. Some of them now favor the theory that the basic constituents of matter are really twelve-dimensional objects called membranes.

Some of these things—superstrings, imaginary time, and so on—may eventually turn out to be real. It is not inconceivable that some future experiment might indirectly conform their presence. After all, although we can't see virtual particles either, we can observe their effects. However, at the moment, it would not be unfair to say that a great number of theoretical physicists and theoretical cosmologists are busy creating new universes of the mind. Their theories may be mathematically consistent, but there is no guarantee that the theoretical entities they deal with correspond to anything that exists in reality.

It appears that physics has gone a step farther than mathematics. Mathematicians may have differing views abut the true nature of their subject. But physics has introduced ideas that are clearly the creations of our minds.

PHYSICS IN THE TWENTIETH CENTURY

The science of physics evolved rapidly during the twentieth century. I certainly wouldn't presume to judge whether the theoretical cosmologists and the superstring/membrane theorists are on the right track. However, it is obvious that the things they do bear little resemblance to the research that was done in the years following the beginning of the century. In 1900, and for a number of years thereafter, it was experiment that suggested the paths that theoretical physicists should follow. Planck formed his quantum hypothesis because it seemed to be the only way to explain certain experimental facts. Bohr's theory of the atom was designed to explain known facts about the behavior of atoms. Quantum mechanics was developed because physicists realized that there were circumstances under which Bohr's theory failed. Even the special theory of relativity, as Einstein was fond of pointing out, was designed to explain accumulated experimental knowledge.

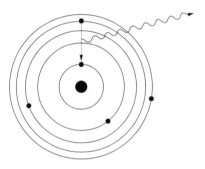

FIG. 4: *Bohr's quantized atom. According to Niels Bohr's theory of the atom, the negatively charged electrons moved around a positively charged nucleus in circular orbits. When an electron "jumped" from a higher orbit to a lower one, a ray of light was emitted. Although this picture has been replaced by the more complicated one of quantum mechanics, physicists still sometimes use it because of its simplicity.*

But then, gradually, some of the theoretical work in physics began to take on a different character. Einstein seemed to know intuitively that the universe could be based on certain mathematical structures, and not on others. If a theory were mathematically elegant, if it were based on the simplest possible mathematical assumptions, then—in his mind—it had to be true. What is amazing is that he so often turned out to be right. There were a few simple experimental confirmations of general relativity in his day. But alternative explanations could not be entirely ruled out until a series of very accurate tests of general relativity were made in the 1960s, after Einstein was dead. Of course Einstein was not always right. Nowadays most physicists agree that his criticisms of quantum mechanics were wrongheaded. A great deal of experimental and theoretical work has been done since Einstein's day, and the position that he took seems to be untenable.

Sometime around 1970, theoretical scientists began to venture into new areas of thought. Experiment was gradually left behind and, finally, the connections were severed almost completely. Theoretical physicists had gone from interpreting experiments that were performed in the laboratory to creating imaginative new universes.

Even an incorrect theory can lead to new insights. Once we discover *why* it was wrong, we have a better idea of what a correct theory should be like. Thus I could hardly object to the often very wild speculation that goes on in the field of cosmology these days. After all, even if we cannot tell what is true, we still learn something when we determine what *might* be true. And once we know this, we often discover new paths to explore.

In any case, my topic here is not so much contemporary science as the scientific imagination. I hope I have shown that, although scientists imaginative abilities are no better or worse than they were a century ago, the objects of the scientific imagination have changed. Scientists used to try to explain the world. Now they often create new, possible, worlds instead. Much of contemporary physics and cosmology is Kantian almost by definition.

APPENDIX

As strange as it sounds, the question of the nature of mathematics is one that we might eventually be able to answer experimentally. It has always been assumed that if we were to come into contact with an extraterrestrial civilization, we could begin to establish contact with them by transmitting some of the basic theorems of mathematics.

But of course this idea depends upon the assumption that their mathematics would necessarily be like ours. If the Platonists are correct about the nature of mathematics, there would be no problem; our extraterrestrial neighbors could not help but discover the same mathematics that we do. But suppose the Kantian view is correct. If our hypothetical extraterrestrials had minds that were unlike ours, they might create entirely different kinds of mathematics.

Unfortunately we have not discovered any extraterrestrial civilizations to communicate with. For all we know, this might never happen. However, the development of high speed computers has raised the possibility that, before too many years pass, we might be able to create intelligent life.

I am not speaking here of the field known as *artificial intelligence*. Scientists in this field attempt to program computers to behave intelligently. Almost by definition, the artificial intelligence that they seek to create would be very much like ours. After all, they typically try to see if they can get computers to do some of the things that the human mind can do. In fact, there already exist programs that can prove theorems in mathematics. *Our* mathematics, of course.

But suppose artificial electronic life were to develop intelligence through natural selection. There would be no guarantee that this intelligence would be anything like ours. In fact it might be so different that we would have difficulty understanding, or possibly even recognizing it. Among other things, we might find ourselves confronted with a mathematics that was completely alien to us. And if this were to happen, it would disprove the Platonist view of the subject.

This is not as far fetched as it may sound. In 1990, University of Delaware biologist Tom Ray created an artificial world, called Tierra, inside a computer in which computer viruslike organisms could reproduce, mutate, and evolve. Because they lived in a relatively simple environment, these digital creatures did not evolve a great deal of complexity. But evolution was observed to take place.

As I write this, Ray and other scientists are creating artificial organisms that are designed to live on the Internet. They can move from one computer to another as they explore their new worldwide environment. Ray and his colleagues hope that the richness of the environment will allow evolution to reach high levels of complexity, leading eventually to the evolution of intelligence.

The idea is not an unreasonable one, since evolution can progress much more rapidly in an electronic environment than it does in the natural world. In the original Tierra experiment, for example, electronic parasites that preyed on the life with which Ray's electronic world had been seeded evolved in a matter of hours. The organisms that harbored the parasites evolved defenses against them almost as rapidly.

If intelligent organisms do evolve in the Internet experiment (which will continue for a numbers of years, possibly indefinitely), their thought processes would probably not resemble ours. After all, they live in a world where there is no physics and no chemistry. And the geometry of their universe is not like ours. That is, once they begin to inhabit a computer they do not move around in a two- or three-dimensional space. Their *space* is one in which the only variable is the amount of energy they can obtain from the computer's CPU (central processing unit). Thus if they did ever develop Euclidian geometry (to cite just one example), it would necessarily be a very abstract subject that was not related to their perception of space. One is thus entitled to ask the question: If we transmitted a mathematical theorem to them, would they understand it? Or, if they proudly gave us a theorem in their mathematics, would we know what they were talking about?

No one knows the answers to these still-hypothetical questions. I, for one, wouldn't even attempt to make a guess. But I look forward to finding out what electronic intelligence will be like, if indeed it does evolve.

By the way, you don't have to worry about finding Ray's electronic creatures in your computer. They can't live in it if you don't provide an environment by installing Ray's program. On the other hand, if you are interested, the program is available free to the general public, and it will run under the current version of Windows. The easiest way to get it is to go to Ray's website at: www.hip.atr.co.jp/~ray/tierra/tierra.html. Or try the Santa Fe Institute's site at: www.santafe.edu. Among other things, the Institute acts as a repository for artificial life information and software.

INDEX